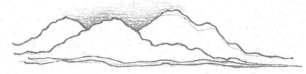

Bean Camp to Brior Patch

Life in the POW Camps of Korea and Vietnam

John N. Powers

Second Edition

ISBN 978-0-615-42731-7

Library of Congress Control Number: 2011904050

Published by
Cronin Publications
P.O. Box 151
Wittenberg, WI 54499
croninbooks.org

Cover Art by Cathy Kirk

Book layout and construction:
Graphic Liaisons llc
C. Potts Design
Waupaca, WI
graphicliaison@mac.com

Printed in the USA by
Worzalla
Stevens Point, WI
worzalla.com

Dedication

On 8 December 1941 two hundred and three US Marines (including their Navy medical team) were captured in China and spent from that day until 15 September 1945 as slave labor in various prisoner-of-war camps in China and Japan. My wife's father, Platoon Sergeant Harold A. Hoffman, was one of those men. As with many POWs, he died young. Contact with the survivors in 2001 brought to my attention the fact family members know little about the POW experience. The result was the web site www.northchinamarines.com. While researching the North China Marines I was asked by the American Ex-POW Organization to write about the Korean and Vietnam POW experience. That work led to the realization the same need existed for a source of information for families of POWs from those wars. Too many families of too many POWs know too little about the story. Too many children and grandchildren can recite details about the life of an actor or athlete but know nothing about the details of their father's or grandfather's life while a prisoner-of-war.

I spent years in the classroom trying to find material to help my students understand their history. You will not find any mention of prisoners-of-war in your child's history text-book. It is my hope that after reading this book you will donate it to your local high school library to help our youth understand what service to your country, and sacrifice for your country, really mean.

By trying to understand what they endured we honor those who sacrificed so much.

Acknowledgments

Many thanks are due to Joan Brahmer, Jody Moegenburg, Margaret Nelson, and Shirley Schmidt for their editing skills and welcome advice.

Table of Contents

Introduction

What you are about to read is more a document than a book. It is modeled after the manner in which post-war reports on Japanese Prisoner-of-War (POW) camps after World War II were written. Those reports are commonly referred to as the Gibbs reports after John M. Gibbs, the author of those documents on POW camps in Japan. Reports on Japanese POW camps in China were written by Captains James Norwood and Emily Shek. Similar reports were never created on POW camps in Korea and Vietnam. The information provided here fills a sixty year gap in the records. There is no other single source in which this information can be found.

The purpose of this document is to present a general overview of the POW experience and the camps they were held in. Books written on the topic almost always present the story of one individual. That means the focus is a narrow one. By presenting a broad overview of the camps and conditions in those camps this document allows family members to better comprehend what their grandfather, father, or brother endured as a prisoner-of-war. It is for those family members this book was written.

The use of names is limited by design. Again, the focus is on the camps and conditions in those camps, not individual POWs. In a few cases concerning some of the smaller camps in Vietnam, the names of POWs known to have been in the camp are listed. It is important to remember that when those lists appear, they very likely do not have the names of all the prisoners who were held at that location. Listing the names of POWs in specific camps in Korea is almost impossible. Close to half of the prisoners died that first winter. The Koreans and Chinese destroyed any lists they discovered. In both Korea and Vietnam POWs were frequently moved from one camp to another. The lists available today were almost always compiled after the war and do not include everyone held at each location. The Korean EX-POW organization and the NAM-POW organization both have some camp rosters but none are complete.

The average reader will find some parts of this book difficult to accept as truth. Many POWs quit talking about their experience because people don't believe them when they describe what their life as a prisoner was like. We live in a comfortable world and face few long-term hardships. Not many of us have had to watch our friends freeze to death or die of starvation and wonder if we were next. Not many of us have spent years in a darkened cell eating food with feces and dirt deliberately added to it. Not many of us have been kept for months in cages too small to stand up in. Prisoners-of-war in Korea and Vietnam dealt with these circumstance and more. By making an effort to understand their experience we honor their sacrifice.

Part I

Chapter One

Korea Background

The Korean War began on the morning of 25 June 1950 when North Korean troops crossed the 38th parallel and invaded South Korea. The South Korean Army was outnumbered by about two to one. Less than 500 Americans were stationed in South Korea at that time in various advisory capacities.

Within three days of crossing the parallel, North Korea had taken Seoul, the capital of South Korea. By August, South Korean and US forces were pushed back to the Pusan Perimeter on the southeastern coast of the Korean peninsula. They remained there until 15 September when the landings at Inchon were followed by the breakout from Pusan on 16 September. On 27 September Seoul was recaptured by UN forces. Less than two weeks later US and South Korean (ROK) forces crossed the 38th parallel and headed toward the North Korean capital of Pyongyang. The push north continued until November when Chinese Communist troops entered the war. By the end of November UN forces were again in retreat southward. Seoul fell to Communist forces for the second time on 4 January 1951.

By the end of January 1951 UN forces were again attacking northward, reaching Seoul in the middle of March. Just over a year after the start of the war, on 10 July 1951, armistice talks began. These talks continued for two more years with little change in the amount of territory held by either side. An armistice was signed on 27 July 1953. From 20 April through 3 May 1953 Operation Little Switch took place. During this time sick and wounded POWs were exchanged with 684 UN prisoners returned by the Chinese. Remaining prisoners were exchanged during Operation Big Switch from 5 August through 23 December 1953. The North Koreans did not allow any Red Cross involvement until the prisoner exchange had already begun after the armistice.

There are some serious misconceptions concerning the Korean War. The first is that the Korean War was lost. In fact, not only was the North Korean Army defeated, but the Chinese Army as well. US forces fought against both armies as part of the United Nations effort to drive them out of South Korea. The United Nations passed several resolutions pertaining to the invasion of South Korean territory. The first was Security Council Resolution 83, passed on 27 June 1950. It recommended that members of the United Nations furnish assistance to South Korea to repel the attack by the North Koreans. The resolution called for North Korea to withdraw its forces to the 38th parallel. No UN resolution called for the taking of any North Korean territory. The United Nations, with the bulk of the forces coming from the US, won the Korean War. Proof of that can be seen by comparing life in South Korea today to life in North Korea.

American troops involved in the Korean War paid a price for their participation. They were seen by many back home as having lost the war. The American public was used to World War II style battles and victories. Korea was different. Americans did not see that difference and few were directly involved in the war. This made it easy for the general public to accept the misconception we had lost the war. It was also easy for them to accept the misconception that Americans who fought there must have been of lesser quality than American troops in previous wars.

A tremendous price was paid by those Americans who became prisoners of war in Korea. First, a larger percentage of American POWs died as prisoners in Korea than any war since the American Revolution. Second, the folks back home assumed most of the POWs who survived had cooperated with the Communists. Albert Biderman talks about American POWs being subjected to the propaganda of the Communists as prisoners during the war and then being subjected to the propaganda of fellow Americans after their return home. He says, "The theme of this propaganda was that there had been wholesale collaboration by the American prisoners with their Communist captors…" and that this behavior showed the American military man to be weak. This misconception came from some magazine articles and two authors whose writings were accepted as being well researched. In fact, those writings were full of gross errors. Those writings, and those misconceptions, led to many returning POWs being investigated by the FBI. Some of those investigations continued into the 1960s.

Some writings accepted as fact by the American public stated that thirty-three percent of US POWs were guilty of minor collaboration and fourteen percent had seriously collaborated with the enemy. A study for the Secretary of Defense, however, found only 192 cases of what the report termed "improper behavior." That amounts to just over four percent of all American POWs. Only fourteen of those were actually brought to court martial. That amounts to 1/1000th of all American POWs. Yet, over fifty years later, there are still inferences in the media about the large scale "brain-washing" of American POWs in the Korean War. Even the fact so many died as prisoners was held against them - as if they died simply because they were weaker than Americans in previous wars. This remains a terrible injustice to the men who suffered in those POW camps in North Korea.

A common argument found in literature claiming a weakness in American POWs is that fewer British POWs died and fewer collaborated with the Chinese. The actual numbers do not support either of those claims. There were no British troops captured from July through December 1950, during which time almost 4000 Americans were captured. No more than 160 British troops were captured prior to the end of April 1951 when 600 were captured at the Imjin River. Over ninety percent of the US Army deaths occurred among those taken prisoner from July 1950 through April 1951. This means almost all of the dying among American POWs took place prior to the point at which British troops were first captured. British figures give a total of 1148 POWs with a death rate of about fifteen percent. From April 1951 through July 1953 there were 1333 US Army troops captured. Their death rate was under fourteen percent. The survival rate for British and US Army troops captured during the same time period is statistically identical.

A second argument is that far more Americans openly cooperated with the Chinese. Again, the numbers do not support the argument. The British military found twelve percent of their soldiers actively collaborated with the Chinese and eight percent actively resisted. The US Army puts Americans who actively collaborated at fifteen percent and those who actively resisted at five percent.

American POWs are constantly insulted in literature, accused of dying in such large numbers because they simply gave up. The term "give-up-itis" appears frequently in discussions about Korean War POWs. Until the spring of 1951 the POWs were fed primarily a diet of corn or sorghum, also known as millet. Frequently meals were raw, uncooked corn or sorghum. Soon after their initial capture, many of the prisoners developed chronic diarrhea. They assumed it was because they drank water that had not been boiled (they had no means to boil it) or used contaminated snow to quench their thirst. Those assumptions are valid, but it also happened because their diet of corn and sorghum caused the disease pellagra. The first symptom of pellagra is diarrhea.

Pellagra is defined by four Ds: diarrhea, dermatitis, dementia, and death. It is a systemic nutritional wasting disease first recognized in the early 1700s. The disease is caused by a lack of niacin. For two hundred years the disease was a major problem for poor peasants in Europe who subsisted on a diet of corn. It continues to be a problem for many poor in India who subsist on sorghum/millet. The POWs in Korea were partially correct when they assumed a lack of adequate boiling of the corn caused their intestinal problems. The inadequate boiling left sharp edges on the husks that irritated the walls of the intestinal tract, but it also led to a more serious problem. The grain must be soaked for a long period of time to break down the outer shell and release the niacin within the corn.

First the body produces hunger-suppressive endorphins. Body chemistry tells the brain the body is not hungry. The individual becomes weak, apathetic, disoriented, falls into a coma, and dies. All of this can happen in less than two months. What appeared to be POWs giving up were symptoms of the disease they contracted as a result of their diet. When more rice was introduced into their diet and the prisoners themselves took over food preparation, the death rate dropped to almost zero. In addition to pellagra the POWs had to deal with bronchitis, dysentery, fevers, infectious hepatitis, nutritional edema, pneumonia, scurvy, and tuberculosis.

A third misconception about the Korean War is that no Americans escaped from the POW camps in North Korea. This supposedly proves the POWs in Korea were not of the caliber of Americans in previous wars, specifically World War II. In that war, American POWs held by the Germans or Italians could pass as Germans or Italians, both in looks and language. Except for a small number of American POWs who were of Oriental descent, this was not the case in Korea. Records show Americans did escape from the North Koreans or the Chinese before they reached the permanent camps on the Yalu. The US Army lists 670 escapes where an individual reached US forces. The US Army lists 5,961 as the total of Army personnel captured. That means, according to official figures, at least eleven percent of the POWs escaped during the Korean War. Figures for World War II and Vietnam give escapes at two percent and four percent respectively. These numbers show there was actually a higher percentage of successful escapes on the part of Americans in Korea than in any other war. It is true no Americans successfully escaped from the permanent camps along the Yalu. However, there were hundreds of attempts, including individuals who made multiple escape attempts from those permanent camps. In 1952 there were at least forty-one escape attempts from Camp 2 alone. This amounts to twelve percent of the POWs in just one camp. All of the permanent camps had the Yalu River and China to the west and endless mountain ridges in all other directions. These ridges ranged from 500 to 1000 feet high and more, physical barriers equal to any barbed wire fence or brick wall. Crossing one or two was possible, but sooner or later exhaustion and hunger forced any escaped POW to take risks which led to their re-capture.

Any discussion of Korean War POWs collaborating, or not trying to escape, or dying because they were somehow deficient in character is clearly not based on the facts - and a terrible insult to those Americans held as prisoners in Korea.

Chapter Two

Death Marches and Executions

As early as 5 July 1950 US troops were captured as North Korean forces pushed south. By the end of the war 7,245 Americans had been captured (93% US Army, 3% US Air Force, 3% US Marine Corp, 1% US Navy). Of this number 2,847 died as prisoners of war. Many historians feel that at least 1,000 Americans were executed shortly after their capture in the early months of the war and are not included in the official figures. In either case, Americans held as prisoners of war in Korea died at a rate far above POW deaths in every war since the American Revolution. The numbers above give a death rate of thirty-nine percent. Add one thousand to each of the above figures and the death rate was over forty-six percent. There was one mass grave discovered holding 7,000 South Korean bodies. How many Americans were buried in unmarked graves? Throughout the war American bodies would continue to be found in shallow graves, hands wired behind their backs, killed execution style with shots to the back of the head. If we assume just one-quarter of the 8,000 still missing were captured, the overall death toll for POWs rises to fifty-two percent. (Accurate figures are hard to obtain when looking at Korean War POWs. Different sources frequently cite different numbers. For every statistic used here you will probably be able to find another.)

Right from the beginning of the war American POWs were treated differently than in any previous war. From July to November 1950 there were seven documented incidents in which a total of over 200 American prisoners were very deliberately executed by the North Koreans. The number of executions with no surviving witnesses we can only guess at.

On 5 July 1950 an American officer observed North Korean troops as they shot and bayoneted thirty-three wounded Americans in an aid station. The officer was himself captured shortly after.

On 17 July 1950 North Koreans overran a group of about twenty American wounded. They were being cared for by a surgeon wearing a Red Cross armband and a chaplain wearing a cross. All were immediately shot. The surgeon survived.

In mid August a group of about forty-five American POWs was taken to a ravine where they were shot. Their boots had been taken and their hands tied behind their backs. Four survived to tell the story.

In late September about sixty American POWs held at Taejon were forced into ditches with their hands wired behind their backs. They were executed in groups of fourteen at a time.

In mid October twelve American POWs were shot by their North Korean guards while being held in a hut near Naedae. Five of the twelve survived to tell the story.

In late October about 180 American POWs were being sent north from Pyongyang in open railroad cars. A fifth of their group had already died as a result of being marched 250 miles in three weeks. On 20 October the train arrived at the Sunchon tunnel. The prisoners were taken in small groups to nearby ravines - to be fed, they were told. The North Koreans shot sixty-eight of the prisoners. Others died when conditions in the tunnel exacerbated their already serious medical problems. (Many references to this massacre use the date 30 October. Joseph T. Monscvitz, one of the survivors, says it happened 20 October.)

In early November an American patrol was captured near Kaesong. While being marched away they were shot by their guards with no warning. One of the thirteen survived.

In December 1950 five American bodies were found, having been stabbed repeatedly by sharpened bamboo sticks. A medical examination showed no single wound had caused death. They had been tortured, some stabbed as many as twenty times.

In many cases the victims had their hands tied or wired behind their backs. In almost every case the North Koreans checked the bodies for signs of life, then shot or bayoneted any who reacted. Survivors frequently had multiple wounds. These executions were only the beginning.

Those prisoners not immediately executed were marched from their point of capture to temporary holding points. These were not camps but often homes or buildings in small villages, or even caves. They would be held at these locations for a few weeks or a few months, then marched to permanent camps. One American captured at the end of November 1950 did not reach a permanent camp until 25 March 1951. Most of that time was spent being moved, on foot, during the Korean winter, from one place to another. POWs in the Korean War traveled by train, truck, jeep, barge, oxcart, donkey, and in at least one case, on the back of a cow. But most of all they moved from point A to point B on foot. In many cases, on bare feet.

When first captured, it was not uncommon for POWs to have their boots and any heavy outer clothing taken away. The standard food ration was one or two rice balls a day and little water. Medical care was minimal, if any at all. The extreme cold, minimal diet, and lack of medical care for wounds had immediate negative effects on the POWs. When these circumstances forced prisoners to fall behind on forced marches, they were executed. These marches should be as well known as the Bataan Death March, but like most facts relating to the Korean War, the American public is almost completely unaware of these events.

The Tiger Death March is well known to those POWs who survived and to serious students of Korean War POW issues. The name comes from the nickname given to the Korean officer in charge of the group that included military and civilian prisoners. The Tiger Death March began on Halloween 1950, but many of its participants had been captured as early as June. About 80 of the group died before the march began. Prior to that Halloween day they had already experienced lack of food, water, and medical treatment. They had been marched from one temporary location to another and then back again. They had been strafed and bombed by US planes. They had seen fellow POWs beaten and shot. In early September another POW spotted the Tiger Death March group in Pyongyang. He described them as "… ragged, dirty, hollow-eyed men…" wearing what he could barely recognize as American uniforms. Another POW described them as, "… crawling with lice. A large portion of them had no shoes. They wore

(NARA photo.) The photo above shows some of those Americans captured early in the war. Clothing is missing or torn, feet are bare, and they are very thin. These factors alone made surviving the winter very difficult.

light-weight summer fatigues." The sick, "...walked like figures in a slow-motion film..."

On 9 October the group left the town of Manpo on the Yalu River in northwestern North Korea. From 9 October to 31 October the American military POWs slept in fields, often as it snowed. On the first day of the march the Tiger shot an American officer because the POWs were not keeping up with the pace he demanded. This execution took place in front of the entire group as an example of what would happen to others who failed to keep up. The prisoners slept in the open or were crammed into unheated buildings. This went on for nine days, crossing a mountain pass in the process. On some days they received raw corn, the same corn normally given to farm animals. Other days they got nothing. Those who could not keep up were executed by the guards. Those executed included a seventy-six year old nun. Others froze to death at night. About ninety were executed or died on the

March, a death rate twice that of Americans on the Bataan Death
March. Unable to recover from the effects of the March, POWs continued to die. Within a week and a half after 9 November, twenty-four
more POWs died. By March 1951 the death toll was twenty-one of
fifty-nine civilians, 400 of 650 enlisted men, and twenty-three of
thirty-five officers. Lasting nine days, with little or no food, covering
100 miles, sleeping in the snow, crossing mountains, executions by the
guards, all resulting in a death toll of at least fifty percent, the Tiger
Death March should be embedded in the American mind as firmly as
the Bataan Death March or D-Day. According to a 1994 Rand report,
when this group was finally turned over to Chinese control in October
1951 only 232 were still alive. Those numbers put the final death toll
at seventy percent. (References to the Johnnie Johnson list have 262
alive in August 1953. Some sources list 744 beginning the March, others list 758. It is extremely difficult to get accurate numbers.)

     And there were other death marches. In early 1951 there were
320 American POWs who were marched from a collection point to
Bean Camp. They marched two to three weeks, beginning each day's
march as the sun set and stopping just before dawn. Orders were
given by the Chinese the wounded were not to be carried. The prisoners were fed as the night's march began and when they stopped each
morning. They ate with their hands, some using their caps as bowls.
While marching through South Korea the locals would often sneak
them extra food. Once in North Korean territory the diet changed.
Each meal was the same - cracked corn molded into a ball with soya
bean paste. The corn was not ground and was poorly cooked, leaving
sharp edges which caused more problems when diarrhea set in. They
received water only at dawn. Diarrhea hit them early in the march. If
they had to empty their bowels they would try to move to the front of
the column and squat so they could rejoin as the column passed. If
they were not ready by the time the end of the column passed by the
guards would club them and leave them to freeze. Some POWs got up
from this beating and continued marching-some did not. The lack of
vitamins brought on night blindness, causing some POWs to walk
over the edge of bridges and mountain ledges. During the day they

were housed in huts. Some days not everyone could fit inside and some were forced to stay out in the cold with no fires to help keep warm. Those inside had no fires either, but they did have body heat and were out of the wind. Every evening a few more were dead. The first week of the march they had to perform calisthenics every evening.

One day they were kept in a village which was also a Chinese Army ammunition dump. American aircraft strafed the village, killing some POWs and injuring more. For the last few days of the march their Chinese guards let them carry those too weak to make it on their own. The enlisted men refused to do so, as did the senior officers. The junior officers did what they could. Of the 320 POWs who began the march to Bean Camp, 120 arrived at their destination. That is a death rate of sixty-two percent and does not factor in those deaths after arrival at Bean Camp. History has not even bothered to give a name to this atrocity.

About 900 POWs were marched from Kuna-ri on 4 December 1950, arriving at Death Valley twenty days later. Army doctors in the group estimated twenty-five per cent died along the way.

On 24 April 350 POWs left Bean Camp on a march to Camp 1. The next day another group of 350 left. About 17 May only 210 of the original 700 arrived at Camp 1. Over the next few weeks 100 more were brought into camp. The twenty-two day march led to a death rate of fifty-five percent.

On 20 May 1951 about 500 POWs were marched from a collection point to the temporary holding center at Mining Camp. They marched for forty-six days with little food, shelter, or medical care. Only fifty percent survived the march.

On 16 September 1951 about 160 POWs left their temporary camp on the way to Camp 3. None of them had shoes. Forty seven made it to Camp 3 on 16 October, a death rate of sixty-eight percent.

Before reading further you must realize you will have a difficult time fully understanding the conditions under which these men lived and died. The winter of 1950-51 was extremely cold, with recorded temperatures of thirty and forty degrees below zero. In his book, *About*

Face, David Hackworth (Col. US Army, Ret) discussed that first winter. "It was so bitterly cold you couldn't sleep. You had to keep moving, stomping feet and flexing fingers twenty-four hours a day. Those who didn't were saying good-bye to their hands and feet (and in some cases their lives): for a while every day a couple of men were evacuated because of frostbite-black toes and fingers to be cut off at the hospital...It was a frigid, brutal, soul-destroying time..." Those remarks are in reference to men within the US lines. Remember these remarks when later you read about POWs reaching down and breaking off their own frozen toes. (It is ironic that Hackworth's words can be used to understand why so many POWs died that first winter as he went out of his way to demean those same men, referring publicly to their conduct as "the Korean War disgrace.")

Early in their captivity many of the POWs were fed raw kernels of corn, frequently receiving only two handfuls a day. Many of them had to eat whatever food they were given using their hands as a bowl. If they had a container of some kind to hold their food, they had to use their fingers to eat. These were the same hands and fingers they had to clean themselves with when diarrhea and dysentery hit them early in their captivity. Little water was available to drink, even less to clean themselves. It was common for their captors to take their boots in trade for whatever footwear the Koreans or Chinese had. The difference in physical size between Americans and Asians meant the American POW then had no footwear. Most prisoners were not able to take a bath or cut their hair until the spring of 1951. Lice were impossible to avoid. During that first winter there was seldom any heat source other than body heat and almost no medical care was provided. The dead were stripped of clothing so the living could survive a little longer. Half of those captured in 1950 and early 1951 died by the summer of 1951.

As you read about conditions in the camps remember that a meal—as in "they received two meals a day"—was not the same *meal* we eat. Each meal for the POWs consisted of about two cups of rice or sorghum. After the first year some greens and meat were sometimes added. They would also have a cup of hot water or tea-nothing more.

Use of the term "the hole" is found in reference to just about every camp. The hole was where a POW was held for punishment. The hole was sometimes actually a pit dug in the ground. More often it was a small hut or a room within a building. When in the ground, it was covered over to keep the heat in during the summer and the cold in during the winter. Whatever the pit was, it was meant to be as mentally and physically uncomfortable as possible. The 1954 film, Prisoner of War, starring Ronald Reagan, is probably the only movie about prisoners of war in Korea and is ridiculous in its historical accuracy. It shows a series of six by six two foot deep holes with men in each one moaning, as if lying fully stretched out in a two foot deep hole would cause severe discomfort. Our knowledge of what it meant to be a POW in Korea was so minimal we took the idea of "the hole" to be no more than that. It may be nearly impossible to fully comprehend what these men went through, but we owe them a better attempt to understand than history has given them so far.

Chapter Three

Temporary Camps

After their capture prisoners were usually moved quickly from the area and taken to a temporary camp. Often this meant a march for many days with little food, water, medical care, or shelter. Their guards frequently became lost. Many POWs report passing through the same area twice between capture and arrival at any kind of camp. Some spent weeks and even months marching from point to point and back again with a few days of rest every now and then. Not everyone was taken to a camp. More than just a few were used as truck drivers or cargo handlers and forced to work for their captors. This meant they were targets for UN artillery and planes. Many of these men were last seen by fellow POWs in places like Pyongyang. Most POWs were taken to collection points where they were joined by other prisoners and then marched on to a temporary camp. Prior to January 1951 there were no permanent camps. Even after the establishment of camps 1, 3, and 5, prisoners were still held in temporary camps before being sent on.

Conditions at these temporary camps were terrible. The only improvement over the marches was that some kind of shelter was available. The lack of food, water, and medical care continued. Death tolls were high and by the time the POWs were marched from their temporary camp to one of the permanent camps on the Yalu many were in no condition to survive.

There are over 150 locations listed in official studies of collection points and temporary camps, more than thirty in and around Pyongyang. Many of them are duplicates, called one name by one group of prisoners and a different name by another. Some of them were christened the Bunkers, Death House, Fourteen Day Place, Half-Way House, Pan's Camp, Pike's Peak, and Twin Peaks. Even today the actual location of some of these places has not been determined. Most of these smaller camps held a few POWs for short periods of time. There were several temporary camps that held large numbers of prisoners and were used for months at a time. There are only educated guesses at how many POWs were held in these camps and how many died there. Bean Camp, Mining Camp, The Valley, Kanggye, Death Valley, and the Apex Camps held large numbers of American POWs. The Caves and Pak's Palace held small numbers of Americans at any one time. Camp 12 held a small group on which the North Koreans put extreme pressure to create propaganda material. Pak's Palace was more a North Korean interrogation center than a POW camp.

The term "camp" really just means a location, a place, where the POWs were kept. Often a camp was simply a village of typical Korean homes, called huts by the POWs, where the families were told to get out and the POWs then packed into the homes. The standard home was constructed of mud and straw and had three small rooms. Heat from the kitchen fire was carried to the other rooms through a duct built into the floor. Once prisoners were allowed to have fires in their huts, they had to learn how to build the fire since the floors would heat slowly but could become too hot to lie on. Frequently the village schoolhouse was taken over and used as a barracks. At Bean Camp and Mining Camp the buildings once used to house the mine workers were used to house POWs. The picture most people have of a prisoner of war camp-long buildings surrounded by barbed wire and guard towers-does not apply to POW camps in North Korea.

Bean Camp

(38 42 N 126 21 E) (Bean Camp was sometimes referred to as Mining Camp)

Bean Camp was located about 35 miles by road southeast of Py-ongyang. It was just to the south of the city of Suan. The camp was a major collecting point, a place to hold POWs until the decision was made to send them on to the permanent camps on the Yalu. Prisoners were held here from about January 1951 until the next fall. The camp was controlled by the Chinese.

The barracks were the quarters of miners who had worked there in earlier years. There were about sixteen buildings, 60' by 18', divided into rooms of 10' by 10' with dirt floors. Each room held about fifteen POWs. (Some descriptions say the rooms were 8' by 8' with about ten men per room.) There were three wells in the dirt road which ran through the camp but only one had water. Mountains surrounded the area. The camp held about 900 POWs, mostly American, with some British, Australian, and Turks. Black POWs were kept in a separate company. The bulk of POWs held here were sent to Camp 1 in late April 1951.

The name of the camp came from the soya beans the prisoners were fed. They were fed twice daily at about 9:30 am and 4:00 pm. Each meal consisted of one tennis ball- sized cake of millet, corn, or sorghum, and soya beans. The corn and beans were never cooked properly which caused further problems for those with dysentery. Im-proper cooking left sharp edges which tore at intestinal linings. At night the meal was one grain cake and about a half pint of soya bean soup. Thus the name – Bean Camp. (Confusion arises by some refer-ring to the camp as Mining Camp.) The improperly cooked corn led to pellagra, which caused a number of deaths. The sick were fed a diet of grain with turnips added. The turnips added salt and minerals which all the POWs needed but did not receive. All prisoners had to line up to get their food, even the sick. Some were too sick to leave their bar-racks. If they had a friend who would bring them food, they ate. Food was of poor quality and quantity. At times a count was made in each room to determine how many balls of grain would be given to that room. Prisoners in more than one room kept the body of a dead POW as long as they could to get the extra food.

Medical treatment consisted of a mixture of gun powder and ground dog bones given to some as treatment for diarrhea and iodine applied to some wounds. Close to half the camp developed pneumonia, for which the Chinese did nothing. Some rooms were set aside for the sick. The wounds and the feces attracted hordes of flies. No water was available for bathing.

Slit trenches were provided for latrines. With the large number of prisoners sick with diarrhea and dysentery the whole area was covered with feces. Only one well provided any water. Some prisoners would use that well to clean their feces-covered clothing. The well water soon became worm-infested. Some prisoners would drink from the well without attempting to boil the water. Usually they had no means to boil water anyway. The men were also ridden with lice. Many had arrived at the camp after marching long distances from their point of capture with little food provided along the way. These conditions, combined with food of poor quality and quantity, led to the death of at least thirty percent of the POWs during the short time the camp was used. One prisoner counted 380 graves when he left Bean Camp.

Three times a week prisoners had to read out loud from the Shanghai News and other communist papers. Then they had to discuss what they had read. There was no mail sent or received at Bean Camp. Work consisted of burial details and wood-gathering details. Gathering wood meant a five mile round trip over a mountain pass and bringing back a prescribed amount of firewood. POWs were punished for not carrying enough firewood, for leaving their room in the barracks without permission, or for talking to civilians in the area. Punishment consisted of cutting back on the already inadequate food ration, being placed in isolation, or being forced to stand at attention all day. The latter may seem a mild punishment until you consider the POWs were malnourished, frequently had diarrhea or dysentery, and received beatings when unable to maintain the position of attention.

The Chinese forced officers to remove their insignia. Enlisted POWs were told they did not have to take orders from their officers. A corporal was made the commander of the officers' company in the camp. The officers were carefully watched to ensure they did not communicate with the enlisted. As a result, military discipline did not exist in the camp. Prisoners stole from each other. The cooks, who were POWs but not American, sold extra food, of which there should have been none. The POWs had only the clothes they were captured in. Some had parts of their uniforms, even boots, taken from them at capture. No blankets of any kind were issued at Bean Camp.

The Chinese refused to mark the camp in any way to identify it as a POW camp. They used the town as a resting point for their own troops which brought attacks by American aircraft. The third attack in April 1951 killed about twenty POWs. Two days later the POWs were sent to Camp 1; one group of about 350 left on 24 April and another group of the same size left on the 25th. (See Execution and Death Marches.) Those too sick to move, approximately 130 men, were kept behind. After new prisoners arrived in May, everyone at Bean Camp was sent to nearby Mining Camp. Small numbers of prisoners may have been held at Bean Camp into the fall of 1951. There were about 200 US prisoners held at what they called Camp Suan in July and August of 1953. This could have been either Bean Camp or Mining Camp.

Mining Camp
(38 47 N 126 22 E)

This temporary holding camp was about thirty-five miles east of Pyongyang and six miles north of Bean Camp. Mining Camp held groups of POWs of various sizes from December 1950 until the end of the war. The village was surrounded by hills and a stream ran through the center of town. The village had about 300 Korean homes and a number of large barracks-type buildings which had been used to house the mine workers. Each of the buildings had a long hall running down the center and four or five rooms to each side. The individual rooms measured about 10' by 10'.

Prisoners held here from late December 1950 until June 1951 were kept in two of these barracks with the officers held separately. During this time period there were about 800 prisoners held at Mining Camp with twenty-five or more in each 10' by 10' room. They received two meals of ground corn a day. There was little or no water available and no medical care of any kind was provided. It is estimated about half of this group died. In June most of the survivors were sent to Camp 1 with some of the very ill kept back.

New captures in June and July were brought to Mining Camp next. By September they numbered between 400 and 500, including 100 South Koreans, a few British, French, and Turkish, and the rest American. As always the officers were kept apart from the enlisted. Some of the enlisted talk about being kept in a schoolhouse up on a hill across the stream from the officers' huts. The first bath they were allowed was in a large communal tub holding fifteen men at a time. All the prisoners used the same water and then had to dress in the same filthy clothes they had been wearing since their capture. By the time this group left for Camp 1 on 20 September 1951 about 180 of them had died. One debrief puts the camp population at this time at 300. He says they left for Camp 1 on 18 August in three groups of 100 each. In his group, forty died by the time they arrived at Camp 1 on the 7th of October. Another uses the same estimate of POWs but says he left on 21 September and arrived at Camp 1 on 7 October.

The majority of the deaths were caused by starvation. Meals were usually a watery soup and some days nothing at all. The prisoners received no clothing and no blankets. Latrine facilities were primitive and not adequate for the number of men. Beatings from the guards were common. One prisoner who attempted an escape was made to dig his own grave and then executed in it. Even under those circumstances, another prisoner attempted to escape the following day. Dysentery, beriberi, and scurvy were common. Lice were a constant problem and impossible to control under the circumstances. Political lectures began in all the camps in April of 1951, including Mining Camp.

Those prisoners too sick to make the September 1951 march were kept back. They were joined by a few POWs captured in the fall. In December they were all sent by truck to Camp 5. Eight Americans were held at Mining Camp with thirty South Korean prisoners in July of 1952. With all the buildings available they were still crammed into one 10' by 10' room. They received no clothing or medical treatment. Their two meals each day were boiled rice and cabbage soup.

Not all the POWS were sent to Camps 1 or 5. A few were sent to Pak's Palace near Pyongyang for interrogation and indoctrination attempts.

An officer captured in mid July 1953 was held at what he called Camp Suan from the end of July until 21 August. With him were about 180 enlisted men and a dozen officers. Most of the prisoners were American. He described the food and medical care as "atrocious." This reference to Camp Suan could have been either Mining Camp or Bean Camp.

Death Valley

(40 12 N 125 45 E) (sometimes referred to as Mining Camp or a mining camp)

Death Valley was located in an old mining camp just north of Pukchin, about thirty four linear miles southeast of Camp 5 and eighty miles almost due north of Pyongyang. The valley ran north and south with mountains rising 1,000 feet on both sides. The Chinese controlled the southern part of the camp and the North Koreans the northern part. Farther north up the valley was a base area for North Korean troops. A small stream ran through the valley. The first prisoners arrived here the last week of December 1950. Some estimates put close to 2,500 prisoners held at Death Valley with the eventual death toll at about 700.

The POWs were housed in the former mining barracks. Each had six to eight rooms 10' by 10' in size. There were no real windows and doors, just the openings. Twenty-five to thirty prisoners were packed into each room. They slept in shifts and remained in the rooms as much as possible for the warmth generated by their bodies. If the prisoners did not have lice before they arrived, they did shortly thereafter. Scabies became a problem for most. No clothing of any kind was issued to the prisoners. Many of them were missing boots and coats which had been taken from them when they were captured. The dead were stripped of their clothing to be used by the living. The bodies were then stacked in nearby caves.

It is uncertain if fires were allowed in the barracks. Some say they cooked the meals twice a day in the barracks and that would have supplied some heat for a short time twice a day. Some say once they got to Death Valley fires were allowed, the first heat they had since their capture. Others say no fires were allowed or only the hut for the sick was allowed to build a fire. It is possible that all the statements are true, depending on whether they were officer or enlisted and what individual guards would allow. The fact they had to go into the hills every day to gather wood means fires were probably allowed to at least cook the meals in the barracks.

The POWs were fed about nine ounces of cracked corn or millet a day in two meals. Some days they got nothing. For the first few weeks the food was served into whatever container individuals had. For many this meant cupping their hands or using their caps. Bowls were provided later. The food was seldom boiled long enough and was therefore difficult to digest. No vegetables or salt were provided. The calorie intake was so limited rooms would keep the dead in the room as long as possible so the head count would get them extra food. POWs had to go into the hills every day to gather wood. That three to five mile hike into the steep hillsides burned calories their diet could not replenish. Only once was meat included in a meal when one pig was butchered for the entire camp.

Water was available from the stream but the North Korean troops in the upper part of the valley used the stream as their latrine. With no containers to boil water, and little fuel for fires to boil the water, diarrhea soon became a problem. The latrine provided in the lower camp was simply a low area in the middle of the camp. Because of the food and the contaminated water everyone had diarrhea and dysentery. Prisoners were often unable to make it to the latrine area which resulted in feces everywhere. Washing of clothing was impossible which meant feces was in the rooms. No soap or water was available to even wash their hands. There were no tools other than bare hands to clean up the latrines or bury the dead. The extreme cold, poor diet, and terrible hygienic conditions led to dysentery, severe frostbite, fever, pneumonia, and death. There were five Army doctors in the POW population but they were allowed to do little more than wash old bandages to re-use again and again. Estimates of the number of deaths range from 500 to 800.

In April, political lectures began for those still at Death Valley. Many POWs attended as the room used for these lectures was heated and a single tobacco leaf was given to anyone who attended.

On 21 and 22 January 1951 most of the POWs were sent on foot to Camp 5. Each group numbered about 600 men. According to Dr. William Shadish, in his book *When Hell Froze Over*, each man received a cotton padded coat, a blanket, and a hat when they left for Camp 5. The first group to depart included many sick and wounded. They took seven days to get to Camp 5. Those who left on 22 January arrived at Camp 5 in three days. Many of those who survived the march were so weak they died shortly after their arrival.   About 300 sick and injured were kept back. On 13 May only 109 of that group were still alive when they were sent by oxcart to Camp 5. Eleven died on the ten day march and seventy-five more died within a few weeks of arriving.

The Valley

(40 34 N 125 30 E) (sometimes referred to as Sambokal or Sambakkol)

The Valley was five miles southeast of Camp 5. The first POWs came into the valley about 20 November 1950. Many had been captured at Unsan and marched to Pyoktong but a bombing raid on the town made the Chinese decide to move them to this valley. The valley ran east to west. Officers were held at the east end of the valley, enlisted men at the western end. There were about thirty officers and 720 enlisted men. The Chinese and North Koreans shared control of this camp.

The prisoners were housed in the standard Korean home of three rooms. About twenty men were crammed into each room. They were not given shoes, clothing, or blankets. Many were still wearing summer uniforms and some had no boots. The temperatures were well below zero. No water was supplied. Snow became their water source. No latrines were available. No medical care was provided. Lice, scabies, and fevers were common. Conditions were so bad the guards would hold their noses when they had to enter the huts to conduct head counts.

The enlisted men were required to carry firewood and food supplies from a central supply point back to the camp. Prisoners had to go into the hills to gather firewood. It was primarily used to boil the sorghum they were fed. At times they got only whole kernel corn. The daily food intake was about 400 grams, undercooked and lacking in protein. If heat was available in the huts it was only when the two meals a day were cooked. Dried corn stalks were given to some of the POWs to be used as bedding. They searched through the stalks for any ears of corn they might find to eat. One day in late November nine heads of cabbage were boiled to make soup for approximately 500 prisoners.

The two senior officers at Valley Camp made a strong effort to instill discipline among the POWs, even ordering the men not to discuss food. Through their leadership, only ten to twenty-five deaths occurred among approximately 750 prisoners.

The Valley camp was closed on 20 January 1951 and the POWs sent back to Camp 5 at Pyoktong.

Kanggye
(41 02 25 N 126 39 08 E)

The Kanggye camp was in a valley a few miles north of the city of Kanggye. There are some references to Kanggye as Camp 10 (see *Remembered Prisoners of a Forgotten War* and *No Mercy: No Leniency*). Some 250 to 300 of the POWs captured in the Chosin area in December 1950 were held here. They arrived the third week of December after a two week march. The prisoners were housed in Korean homes, usually referred to as huts by the POWs. The standard home had two rooms and a small kitchen area. The Korean families had to give up one room for the POWs, who slept ten to twelve per room with their heads to the wall and their legs overlapping. The ondol, or underfloor, heating system of the homes meant the rooms were heated for at least a few hours each day when the family was cooking. The only work detail for the POWs was to gather wood for heating the huts. The steep mountainsides, the weight of the logs, and the poor diet did not make this an easy task. Meals consisted of sorghum with rice added every tenth day. Soy beans and pork were periodically added to the two meals a day.

Medical treatment was minimal, with aspirin being the most modern. A pen-knife was used to remove a bullet from one POW. Scraping dead flesh from frozen toes and removal of those toes was the most common treatment. Some of the very sick were removed from the camp and sent elsewhere for "treatment." Approximately twenty-five POWs died at Kanggye. It is not known if the deaths among the sick removed from camp are included in this figure. Those few who came back from the "hospital" said it was a bombed out building and medical care was almost non-existent. The Chinese medics at the main camp were in reality medical students who were "volunteered" for duty in Korea. They seemed to try but were given almost no medicines or medical equipment.

On their arrival the POWs were given haircuts and a few razors provided for all to shave. Standard padded Chinese uniforms and winter hats were issued. (Some individuals deny this clothing was issued. Numerous sources discuss being issued trousers, jackets, and hats.

Debriefs from prisoners held at Camp 1 make reference to being able to identify the POWs who had been at Kanggye by their Chinese uniforms). Some say the food was inadequate; others say it was the same as that eaten by the Chinese guards. A detailed Marine Corps study says meals were the same as that of the Chinese. This would make both groups correct, as westerners were accustomed to an entirely different diet. There was a distinct difference in the treatment of the POWs at Kanggye and that in other camps at the same time. The death rate alone demonstrates that. There was almost no mistreatment by the guards and haircuts, shaves, and clothing issue did not happen in other camps until late spring of 1951. Other large groups of prisoners captured at the same time at Chosin were held between Chosin and Kanggye. Their treatment was the same as at other POW camps at that time. The group in Kanggye was deliberately treated differently.

The reason for this difference is that Kanggye was an experiment in "re-education" on the part of the Chinese. These were some of the first UN troops captured by the Chinese. Most POWs up until this time had been captured by the North Koreans. The prisoners at Kanggye were the first to experience this Chinese attempt at re-education. Right from the beginning the POWs were told they would be released if they cooperated. Lectures were given in the huts. Instructors would sit in the open door and talk for hours. The prisoners just wanted them to go away so they could close the door again and get warm. Eventually the squad leaders had to lead the lectures. They would watch for any Chinese approaching the hut and then pretend to be seriously discussing some issue. Written responses were required to questions about prisoner opinions on various articles in Communist papers. Group lectures were given in a large barn. During these lectures the senior ranking officer was able to pass on orders and give some guidance on how to react to the Chinese demands for written statements.

Since the prisoners were told they would be released if they demonstrated some signs of cooperation, they did so. The senior officer made it clear this cooperation was to be as limited as possible. A small handful wrote articles for a camp newspaper-New Life. The majority of the POWs, however, soon learned to "cooperate" by not arguing with Chinese during the lectures they were forced to attend. When first questioned about their daily life at home the POWs would talk about owning cars, eating at restaurants, going to movies-a completely accurate description of their lives. The Chinese had been fed so much propaganda about the average American being so poor in comparison to the rich capitalists on Wall Street they could not comprehend what they were hearing. They called the POWs liars and said they must learn the truth. When the prisoners quit arguing with the long-winded lecturers the Chinese saw this "cooperation" as a direct result of their "re-education" efforts. They actually believed they had changed the political views of a large percentage of the POWs at Kanggye. They made the assumption that same level of change would be attainable from any and all UN troops they captured. After the camp was closed they prepared a document describing how POWs could be manipulated, based on their "findings" at Kanggye. That document emphasized the POWs fear of death and of not returning home, and suggested severe treatment could soften them up for "re-education." The Chinese attempt at re-education began in all camps the very next month. It took them another year to realize that, except for a small handful of POWs, their attempts were futile.

In early March 1951 the experiment was over and Kanggye was closed. The prisoners were sent by train to Pyongyang. From here the majority were sent on to Camp 1. About sixty were separated from the group and told they were to be freed. This group was then marched east to the Wonsan area on the coast. On 5 April they were sent south to the Chorwon area. Here they were split again. One group was used for a while to greet new prisoners. At the end of May nineteen of this group were abandoned by their guards near UN lines with plenty of propaganda leaflets. The remaining eleven were rejoined with the larger group of thirty. This group was then marched from one location to another, arriving in the general vicinity of Pyongyang and Mining Camp in August. While there, nine of the POWs attempted an escape. In mid-October they left Pyongyang en route to Camp 1, arriving thirteen days later on about 25 October.

There are references to other temporary camps near Kanggye or between Kanggye and Chosin. One debrief refers to Valley # 1 (also known as Teksil-li) being about four miles northeast of the Chosin reservoir.   About 300 POWs were held there from 3 Dec 1950 to 24 Jan 1951. At that time they were marched to Camp 1, arriving at the end of March. Teksil-li was actually northwest of Chosin, about half-way between the Chosin Reservoir and Kanggye.

Another debrief refers to a camp northwest of Chosin. Here they were kept in Korean homes, each with a six-foot wooden fence on three sides. They slept on the floor of the huts. Medical treatment was limited to periodic visits by a North Korean nurse who would change bandages on wounds by creating new bandages from the linings of POW parkas. She also removed frozen toes and fingers with a pocket knife. At first they had Chinese guards, then North Korean guards. On 21 March at least some of the American POWs held here were sent to Camp 5, arriving the first week of April.

It is possible both POWs were talking about the same camp, but details provided are not enough to determine if that is the case.

Apex Camps – Camp 7
(41 44 N 126 52 E)

The Apex Camps were the three separate camps the civilian and military POWs were held at in the year immediately following their participation in the Tiger Death March. These camps were the farthest north of all the POW camps and held only the Tiger Death March prisoners. They are called the Apex Camps because of their location on a large point, or apex, of North Korean geography. The third camp of the three, An-dong, is also referred to as Camp 7. They were held at Chunggang-jin from 9 to 16 November 1950. Next was Hanjang-ni from 17 November 1950 through 27 March 1951. Finally they were held at An-dong from 27 March to 10 October 1951. All three of these camps were controlled by the North Koreans.

The group arrived at the village of Chunggang-ni on 8 November after ninety died on the movement from Manpo on foot (Tiger Death March). The majority of those who died had been executed for failure to keep up with the pace of the march. During their week-long stay at Chunggang-ni, the prisoners were housed in a schoolhouse. The civilians were given straw to sleep on; the military POWs slept on the bare floor. The civilians had one stove in the doorway separating the men from the women. The run-down condition of the building meant you had to be near the stove for any heat. The military POWs had only body heat to keep them warm.

The group was told their poor health was their own fault – they were not taking proper care of themselves. As a remedy they were forced to perform calisthenics for at least a few mornings after their arrival. The only medical care was that provided by a Korean nurse and "doctor." These individuals had almost no medical supplies and limited medical knowledge. The two doctors among the prisoners were not allowed to work as doctors, only to carry a small medical bag for the nurse. The military POWs had only the clothing they were captured in. Most of them were wearing summer uniforms. Some had no shoes and some no jackets. Lice were a serious health problem. Keeping them under control required about two hours a day of stripping down piece by piece and killing all the lice found in the seams of their clothing.

The cold and the starvation diet made this a risky procedure.

Food was the equivalent of one standard water glass full of millet per day, divided into two meals. Until the prisoners were allowed to prepare their own meals the food was poorly cooked. Even when they were allowed to prepare their own meals, they had to improvise a kitchen and learn how to properly cook the grain. One of the civilians recalls seeing POWs steal frozen cabbage leaves to add to their diet. Since the well in the schoolyard was dry, water had to be brought from the Yalu on carts pulled by POWs. They would be soaked from the splashing of the water from the barrel in the cart.

Chinese troops were constantly moving through the area, and that attracted US aircraft. The village was strafed and bombed during the week the prisoners were held there. Four civilians and twenty-four of the military POWs died at Chunggang-ni.

On 16 November the group was marched northeast to Hanjang-ni, some still in bare feet. The fifty-one civilians were put into one Korean house. The military POWs were put in other Korean houses and the schoolhouse. The Korean homes had heated floors provided the prisoners had enough wood to burn and were allowed to have a fire for heat. The schoolhouse had little or no heat. In all cases the prisoners slept on the floor.

There was little mixing allowed, even with prisoners in neighboring huts. The guards would escort any prisoners outside their huts. Work details were required to haul water, to pick up bundles of wood and the day's food from a central storage point, and to grind the grain. During these details the prisoners were able to exchange information, especially while getting water from the well about 100 yards away. Frequently the water detail would have to stand in the frigid cold while the guards chipped the ice from the well to get at the water. Their minimal clothing made this a very unhealthy activity. No fires were allowed during daylight hours. The guards were concerned smoke would attract the attention of US aircraft. The water detail had to wait until late evening to thaw out and dry their clothing.

Some sources list 203 military and three civilian deaths at Hanjang-ni, others list 222 as a total. Medical care was almost non-existent. Certain houses were designated as hospitals. For the civilians this was a ruined hut. The room used for patients had only a sack for a door and no heat. The condition of the hut meant no fire could be built so food had to be prepared elsewhere. By the time the food got to those in the hospital it was always cold. Temperatures dropped as low as forty below zero at night. Patients slept on the floor on one straw mat, covered by another. The walls would be covered with frost. The prisoners constantly tried to hide any signs of illness from the guards so they would not be sent to the hospital. Almost all those sent to these "hospitals" died there. Many of the military POWs died when flu hit them. Already weakened by months of marching across Korea, their starvation diet, the severe cold, constant diarrhea, and pellagra, too many prisoners had no reserve left when hit by the flu. After November the ground was too frozen to bury the dead.

Most of the military POWs had not had a bath or change of clothing since they had been captured six months earlier. Dysentery was common. Repeatedly having to leave their shelter and step into the frigid night further weakened individuals. Permission had to be granted by the guards before they could leave the hut to use the latrine. Failure to do so often led to being forced to stand in the cold or kneel in the snow with no shirt. At times water was then poured on them. Beatings with rifle butts were common for the slightest of reasons.

Millet continued to be the standard diet at Hanjang-ni. The average was 600 grams per person per day. Meat was included in the meal only a few times and in minuscule amounts. Fish was included only twice. Starting in January 1951 one of the meals each day was usually rice. Soya beans were included when available. As time progressed the prisoners became better at cooking their food, especially learning how to cook the millet so it did not cause diarrhea. A major problem for both heating and cooking was the use of green wood. The local villagers were ordered to supply the prisoners with firewood. They naturally kept what they had gathered prior to the winter months and cut new wood for the prisoners. This green wood made starting and maintaining fires difficult.

At least one military POW was beaten so badly he died. He had torn a board from the fence outside a Korean home to help start a fire. The guards would usually become irate when they found POWs removing wood from structures for any reason. Prisoners were told they must not damage property. The guards had no problem throwing the people out of their homes, but it was important to their ideology that these homes be returned undamaged to the owners.

In January 1951 beriberi appeared among the civilian prisoners. The Koreans supplied soybeans to add to the meals and told the cooks how to prepare them. That solved the beriberi problem. Since the military POWs ate the same or less than the civilians it can be assumed beriberi hit them also.

When an individual died, their clothes were removed to be used by the living. Early in 1951 a standard Chinese winter uniform was issued to each POW. At some point they were allowed to steam their clothing and disinfectant was used on the huts, either because of lice or feces or both.

For a while the military POWs had political lectures about twice a week. In January the Tiger was replaced and gradually beatings by the guards became less common. In early February the diplomats and journalists in the civilian group were removed from Hanjang-ni.

On or about 27 March 1951 the group was moved back down through Chunggang-ni to the third camp at An-dong. This time all the sick were moved in oxcarts. At first the entire group was housed in a fenced-in compound that included a large stone structure of ten or twelve rooms and some nearby buildings. The prisoners thought the larger building had been a hospital. The area measured about 400' by 800' and was surrounded by a 5' high barbed wire fence. In some sources this is referred to as a former police compound.

Prior to this point the civilian and military POWs were not allowed much contact with each other, usually only when on work details. Now they were all in the same compound and mixed more freely. Political lectures continued, but after a while the civilian prisoners were told they would not have to attend. In early May the civilians were moved out of the compound to a house about 100 yards away since the guards felt there was too much intermingling of the civilian and military POWs. After this move the only contact was again on work details such as wood gathering or at the weekly food distribution point. One of the civilian group escaped a while later and was gone three days before recapture.

The weather improved and vegetables started appearing at meals. The normal meal of millet changed to kaoling, or sorghum. A day's portion was still 600 grams but now of equal parts rice and sorghum. Daily activities included the standard tasks of cutting and hauling wood and water and collecting the daily rations from the storehouse. Cooking meant first washing and grinding the grain. Wood-cutting details had the opportunity to pick wild berries, mushrooms, and wild greens. The daily wood-gathering details would consist of 200 to 300 POWs, civilians included, going down the road and into the hills to search for firewood. Oxcarts would be taken along to carry the day's find.

The civilians set up school sessions for the ten children in their group. Once the civilians were put into the hut outside the compound they were allowed more freedom of movement. They would wander into the hills gathering wild plants to add to their daily meals. It was at An-dong the prisoners were finally able to bathe, using the stream. New clothing was issued in the summer.

Although conditions and treatment improved from the winter months the men continued to die. There were sixty-nine military deaths at An-dong and at least one civilian death.

The civilians left An-dong by truck on 9 October 1951 and were returned to Man-po. In August of 1952 they were sent to Ujang and in March of 1953 to Pyongyang, finally being released into Russian care in April. The military POWs were marched to the Yalu on 10 October 1951 and sent down the river on barges. The officers were sent to Camp 2 and the enlisted to Camp 3. One officer died on the way and about ten enlisted died at Camp 3. On arrival at Camp 2 the officers were described as "...scraggy and dirt-grimed, clad in rags, and some of them had skin diseases..."

At least fifty percent of the 845 who began the Tiger Death March died while prisoners, almost all of that number dying at the Apex camps. The dates and the number of deaths used here may not be completely accurate. Different sources use different numbers. Some sources give a figure of eighty-seven civilians beginning the March, others fifty-nine civilians. Some sources say 206 died at Hajang-ni, others say 222. Some sources say sixty died at An-dong, others say sixty-nine. A 1994

Rand report lists only 232 of the original 700-800 alive in October 1951. Those numbers put the death toll at seventy percent.

One source says it was the military POWs who were moved from the compound to the house at An-dong. That is incorrect. One house would not have held the military POWs as they numbered over 300 at that time. Another source says the civilians were moved across the Yalu to a house in Manchuria. That is also incorrect. They were not on the Yalu. There was a small stream that ran through the village of An-dong. The civilians waded across it as they moved from the compound to the house. In their debriefs after the war many of the military POWs seemed to refer to any stream or river as the Yalu.

The Google Earth® photo above shows the location of the three Apex camps.

The Google Earth® photo of An-dong (Camp 7) today shows little change from 1951. The compound where the military POWs were held is easily visible. When the civilians were removed from the compound they waded the stream just to the south and moved to a Korean home another hundred yards or so beyond.

The Caves - Camp 9
(39 04 N 125 56 E)

The Caves were just northeast of Pyongyang very near to Camp 12. They were a series of dark, cold, and wet caves about 100 feet deep. In some cases the entrances were boarded over. Some caves were just large enough to stuff one man inside. The prisoners had to sleep on the ground in the caves even though there were pools of water everywhere. This also served as their drinking water. The area imme-diately outside the entrance to each cave was used as a latrine. Since most prisoners had diarrhea they often did not make it that far. They were fed a small bowl of corn twice a day and given no medical care. Many POWs were simply allowed to die. One POW estimated he saw 300 graves when he was held there. In May of 1951 seventy-seven POWs arrived at the Caves. Six weeks later only twelve of them were alive. In another group of twenty-three, there were no survivors after three weeks. The camp was controlled by the North Koreans.

Pak's Palace
(in the vicinity of 39 09 N 125 48 E)

Pak's Palace was a Korean run camp located a few miles northeast of Pyongyang. It had earlier locations in or around the city but
was finally situated among a large group of buildings including a brick
factory with a 100' high chimney. From this came the name "the
Brickyard." POWs at Pak's Palace were held in four rooms in a long
thatched roofed building. A barbed wire fence surrounded the building
and a courtyard area. A river ran just to the south.

The prisoners were brought there in small numbers to be interrogated by a North Korean team headed by a Major Pak. He was not the
senior officer but handled the interrogations. There were also Russians
in the camp who at times actually conducted interrogations. In many
cases the POWs felt the Russians created the questions asked by the
North Koreans.

The majority of the prisoners brought to Pak's Palace were officers, most of them Air Force officers. They were selected by the Koreans from nearby temporary camps until those camps were, for the most
part, closed down. Prisoners were also brought down to Pak's Palace
from the permanent camps on the Yalu. Interrogations at Pak's Palace
began in February or April of 1951 and continued throughout the war.

While at Pak's Palace the prisoners were forced to work hauling
logs, digging bomb shelters in solid rock, and carrying water and supplies for the Koreans. Their food was the same or of poorer quality
than that in the permanent camps. What little food they received was
frequently withheld when prisoners refused to answer questions. Beatings were common, as were threats of death. Prisoners were often
placed in a hole on the side of a hill with the entrance completely covered. In May of 1951 three POWs escaped and were not caught for a
week or more. When brought back to Pak's Palace, they were placed
in this hole for twenty-six days and forced to use a corner of their
small hole in the ground for a latrine. One POW talks about some
prisoners being housed in a two-story building. The presence of diarrhea and dysentery among the prisoners meant that those on the lower
floor in that building endured dripping urine and excrement. Another

tells of being held in a room so hot they had to stand on a table to keep from burning their feet on the floor.

In June of 1951 there were about thirty US prisoners held at Pak's Palace for three weeks before they were sent on to Camp 5 on 10 July 1951. In October of 1951 about twenty POWs were held there, sixteen of them US. Some prisoners held there in the summer of 1951 talk about frequent deaths among the POW population. A prisoner held there for the month of September 1951 recorded five deaths. In July of 1952 a POW arrived at Pak's Palace. Twelve other prisoners were there when he arrived. At the end of August they were sent on to Camp 5 and on 4 September sent to Camp 2-4.

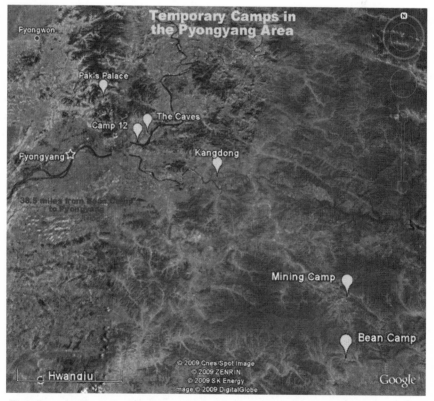

The Google Earth® photo above shows those temporary camps in the Pyongyang area. The linear distance from Bean Camp to Pyongyang is 38.5 miles. Pak's Palace final location was 10 miles northeast of Pyongyang. The actual road miles for POWs being marched from one location to another would have been much more.

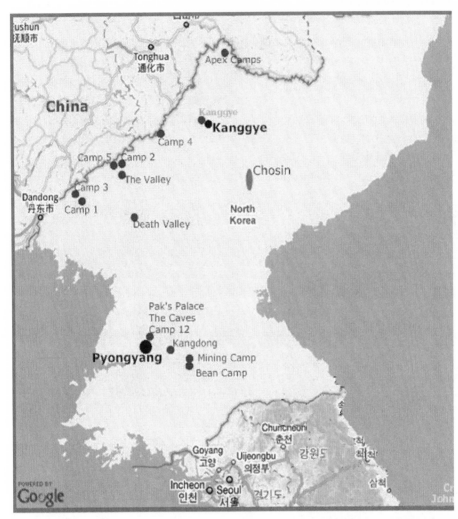

The camps shown above held the bulk of American POWs during the war in temporary and then permanent camps. There were many other temporary camps, or collection points, in which Americans spent some time but their actual locations are hard to determine. In many cases two or three widely separate coordinates are given for what is supposed to be one camp.

Camp 12
(39 03 N 125 54 E)

In January 1951 the North Koreans came to Camp 5 and selected twenty POWs to take back to Pyongyang to what became known as Camp 12 – also known to some as Traitor's Row. Those selected were told they would be broadcasting the names of all the prisoners at Camp 5, making broadcasts to their families back home, or working on body recovery at old battlefields. The two lieutenant colonels that had been the senior officers at The Valley were included in this group. One of them was selected to be the group leader. Camp 12 was moved around the general area of Pyongyang until June 1951 when it was settled just to the northeast of the city in the same general area as Pak's Palace and The Caves.

On their arrival at Camp 12 the prisoners found they were expected to create and sign peace appeals and other propaganda material for the North Koreans. They were told refusal would lead to their execution. Lack of cooperation brought death threats or suggestions they were about to be marched back to Camp 5. In their physical condition that would have meant certain death.

The men at Camp 12 were fed just as poorly as at the other camps. When they balked at producing the required documents or recordings, their meager rations were cut even further. At one point they begged some locals for food and were given a meal of dog soup. They were frequently threatened with transfer to The Caves, a nearby collection point where many POWs were simply allowed to die. Twice some of the Camp 12 prisoners were sent there for a few weeks when they were not cooperative enough. One group spent three weeks at the Caves during which time the 23 Americans already there died. Then the men were sent back to Camp 12.

Even when cooperating, the leaders at Camp 12 were thinking of escape. They drew up detailed plans of rescue by US forces. By this time there were seventy prisoners in or near the camp. The rescue plan called for their recovery by helicopter, an air drop of weapons and equipment so forty men could break out and be rescued nearby, or the dropping of equipment and directions for five men to break out and be rescued on the coast. After the war experts studied the plan and said the rescue of the entire group could have worked. To get their plans out to US forces the men at Camp 12 were forced to appear to be co-operating even more so that one of their group would be freed as a "peace emissary." In the end the North Koreans decided not to release anyone so the plan was never delivered to friendly forces. The senior American officer made three escape attempts after the release was canceled. In early December 1951 Camp 12 was shut down and the men sent back to Camp 5.

There are vague references in debriefs to the location of other temporary camps. In October of 1951 a POW was held at what he called Camp DeSoto. It is described as a real prison in a rectangular area with guard towers at each corner. Another debrief puts DeSoto somewhere north of Kangdong. From there he left for Camp 3.

At the end of May 1951 a POW was held with 300 others at what he called Peaceful Valley. Nearby was the camp called The Pines. Both were supposedly south of Bean Camp. Pan's Camp is referred to as being south of Mining Camp.

Use of the terms "valley," "death valley," "peaceful valley," or "mining camp" are common in POW debriefs. Many of them refer to places which held only a few prisoners for a few days and are obviously not describing a major camp.

Chapter Four

Permanent Camps

Camp 1—Chongsong
(some references use the spelling Changsong)

Camp 1 was established in March of 1951, the first POWs arriving on or about Easter Sunday. Their Chinese guards threw the local villagers out of their homes and installed the prisoners. The name Chang-ni is also used in reference to Camp 1 and actually appears at the location when using Google Earth®. The camp held prisoners until the end of the war.

Location: 40-27-12N 125-12-43E

This was a village on the bank of the Yongju River about 5 miles from where the Yongju fed into a backwater of the Yalu where Camp 3 was located. The area, south southeast of Camp 3, was surrounded by high hills.

Description

The camp consisted of about 60 to 100 typical Korean mud homes with tile or thatched roofs and some barracks-type buildings. Some sources say the number of huts was 200. There were guards at various points around the camp and in the hills nearby. Initially the camp included all ranks, both American and British. In May of 1951, with 600 Americans already there, 300 British prisoners arrived. Some time in May or June the officers and NCOs were put in separate compounds. In October of 1951 the officers were sent to Camp 2 and in August of 1952 the NCOs were sent to Camp 4. At that time black privates and corporals were sent to Camp 5.

At first there were seven companies of POWs. Companies 1 through 4 were American and kept on the west side of the village. Companies 5 through 7 were British and kept on the east side. Prior to the moves to other camps there were approximately 2000 POWs in Camp 1. By the time of the armistice in 1953 the camp held about 1400 POWs.

The POWs were organized into the standard companies of about 200 men, forty men to a platoon, ten to a squad. They were kept in two or three room mud homes with one squad per 10' by 10' room. They slept on the mud floor which they covered with straw mats or empty rice bags. The floor was heated with the standard Korean system, but only when allowed by the guards. Each squad had a Chinese officer assigned to monitor their political "education." There was little or no communication allowed with POWs outside their specific area. Only after the armistice was announced in late July 1953 were the men allowed to visit with other companies, even though they had been in the same camp for two years. By the summer of 1953 some huts had bunk beds.

The 300 British POWs who arrived in May 1951 were kept separate from the Americans, but could easily observe the daily burials in Boot Hill just to the north of camp. In one day they counted thirty-eight burials and estimated 200 died in May and June of 1951. New American POWs arriving at that time were given soap and allowed to bathe in the river, their first opportunity to get clean since being captured months before. Their clothing was replaced with the standard Chinese uniforms.

Food

Until May of 1951 prisoners at Camp 1 were fed sorghum balls with raw soybeans and millet. Then in July of 1951 the diet became sorghum, soybeans, dried fish, and cabbage with a small amount of rice once a week. Meals were twice a day at 8:30 am and then at 4:00 pm. In the summer they were fed three times a day. A noon snack of peanuts was commonly the third meal. Lack of vitamins caused night blindness until turnips and carrots were added to the diet and the night blindness disappeared. In the winter of 1952 a bakery was set up. Barley bread would then replace one meal a day. When the peace talks went well, food quality improved. This meant rice and greens once a week, meat once or twice a week. "Meat" meant a small piece or two in the soup. As peace talks progressed toward the end, they received more rice and sometimes bean curd and canned meat. In his book, *Captured at the Imjin River,* David Green noted the basic diet for his entire time at Camp 1 was "a one pound tin of sorghum or millet twice daily plus the side dish...of about one third of a baked tin of turnip tops or peanuts, a very watery edition of these being issued at about noon."

Medical

Initially there was a high rate of death among the POWs at Camp 1. When they first arrived in March of 1951 many POWs had frozen fingers and toes. Some had no boots. Others had frozen feet and could not fit them into their boots. It was common for frozen toes to break off. There was a "hospital" in a temple on a hill at the edge of the village, viewed by most as a place to die. There was no medical care at all until late 1951. A pill, assumed to be aspirin, was the standard treatment for almost every medical problem. In the summer of 1952 a female Chinese doctor came into the camp. Care improved until her transfer elsewhere. Some prisoners estimated 600 to 800 died through the spring, summer, and fall of 1951. Malnutrition, dysentery, starvation, and lack of medical care were the causes of almost every death. The burial area on the hillside north of the camp was called "Boot Hill." At one point forty-five POWs arrived by truck, probably meaning they were the sick and wounded of a group which had marched to the camp. Within a few weeks forty-three of the forty-five died.

During the summer of 1952 the open ditch latrines caused severe fly problems. POWs were given quotas of flies to kill each day. In the spring of 1953 a more sanitary latrine was built and lime was used.

Treatment

From the beginning the POWs at Camp 1 were regularly lectured and asked to sign peace petitions or make recordings. Starting in the spring or early summer of 1951 they would have to sit out in the open and listen to lectures for two to three hours each morning and afternoon. The POWs were told they were students, not prisoners. If they adopted the wrong attitude, they were Reactionaries. As students they were to "learn the truth." In addition to the lectures each squad was required to respond in writing to questions from their Chinese instructors. Inadequate responses caused lengthy interrogations of the squad leader and frequently led to the squad missing one or two meals. Group lectures were conducted in the open regardless of the weather. The instructors who led these lectures were highly educated Chinese. After the spring of 1952 the lectures were dropped, except for classes a few POWs voluntarily attended. Some prisoners continued to attend these classes for the cigarettes that might be handed out or other favors the Chinese might grant them. Those POWs who cooperated in this way were called Progressives.

The prisoners were given cards to fill out with their biographical information. They were told the senior officer had filled his out, so many POWs did the same. Some used false information or simply refused. In July of 1951 they were ordered to send a telegram of greetings to a peace conference in Chicago. The officers and NCOs refused, but many of the lower enlisted ranks signed. As a result of B-29 strikes in the general area, the Chinese asked for an appeal from the POWs. They were told the name of the village would be used in the letter. Many signed a letter drawn up by the Peace Committee in an attempt to get the camp location to UN forces. After they signed, all references to the camp's location were removed from the letter.

For the October anniversary of the Chinese Revolution, the POWs were told there would be a parade and they would participate carrying banners with peace slogans. In order to eat they had to cooperate, but slogans such as "Down With The Imperialist Warmongers" and "Long Live The Peace-Loving Chinese People" found their way onto the banners missing the words "Imperialist" and "Chinese." The Chinese were very pleased with the creation of a banner with a drawing of a large-breasted female carrying a dove and the accompanying slogan "We Want A Firm Front." It apparently appealed to the Chinese sense of unity. During the parade many yelled insults rather than the slogans they were told to shout. Pictures taken by the Chinese made it look like the entire camp had willingly participated. For the prisoners it simply meant a change from the boring routine of the camp and a meal that included large quantities of potatoes, onions, eggs, and fish. Even with those very welcome rations, two "ungrateful" POWs escaped the following day. In August and September 1951 alone there were at least 13 escape attempts. Summer and fall were the escape seasons.

Those prisoners who did not follow the regulations during the lectures were sent to what some called the Reconsideration Room. This was an unheated space where the prisoner had to sit cross-legged without moving for 16 to 18 hours at a time. There were also small cages in the jail in town where prisoners would be made to stand with their arms through the bars holding a weight. When they dropped the weight, they were beaten. Others were crammed into filthy cells and made to sit upright or stand on one leg. Whenever possible they ignored these instructions, but the guards willingly beat those they caught not following orders. POWs were usually placed in the civilian jail while awaiting trial for crimes such as escaping. Some POWs who attempted escape had their hands tied behind their back with a rope leading from their wrists over a beam and then tied around their neck. This forced them to stand on their toes or strangle themselves. Escapees were sometimes beaten and put into solitary confinement in boxes so small they could not fully stand or stretch out on the floor. About six such cages were kept in one building. Those POWs who experienced these cages called them dog kennels and referred to themselves as the Kennel Club. Some spent months in these cages, only allowed out to use the latrine, and sometimes not even that. During the entire day they were made to sit erect without leaning against any part of the cage. Handcuffs were used on the least cooperative. Some were forced to "stand" in the cage. In a cage 4' high this meant they had to stand doubled over at the waist. The guards were quick to beat them for any infraction, often using their rifles as clubs. In one case, a guard held his weapon by the barrel while pounding on a prisoner. The weapon discharged, killing the guard. That POW was beaten almost continuously for the next five days. Confinement in these cages and beatings would continue until an acceptable confession was written for whatever "crime" had been committed. In the late summer of 1951 one POW, a member of the Kennel Club, was marched some distance from the camp and told that if he did not immediately write a confession he would be shot while attempting to escape. He wrote a confession. Quite a few members of the Kennel Club were eventually transferred to Camp 2-3. During 1952 prisoners would be thrown into the hole from one to four weeks for minor acts such as making a face at a guard. Hard labor was also a common punishment. Beatings, torture, and withholding of food and clothing were standard treatment for individuals who were uncooperative in one way or another.

A reactionary squad of about fifteen POWs was isolated at a Korean farm about a mile from the main camp. Even there, already isolated, they had two solitary confinement rooms. The British referred to this squad as the Slave Labor Unit (SLU). Men in this squad were put to work cutting down trees for lumber or fuel. Some POWs were sent there to serve sentences for various "crimes" and were returned to the main camp when their sentence was completed. These sentences were sometimes handed out at staged trials where the "defense counsel" would argue for severe punishment. Many of the men in this squad were eventually sent to Camp 2-3.

POWs in the main camp also had to go into the surrounding hills to carry firewood for the camp. The Chinese kept track of how much firewood each man brought back to camp to ensure the weight quota was met. Some put this quota at forty to sixty pounds per individual. Gathering firewood could be an eight to ten mile round-trip hike, carrying a heavy load on the way back. Poor diet and lack of medical care made this a dangerous burden so men on the firewood detail were fed three meals a day.

When the peace talks began, cards and ping-pong sets were supplied. Softball equipment was brought in and music was played on loud speakers. Books were made available, most of them communist oriented. After the armistice was signed, Red Cross packages were distributed and life generally improved, but that was only for the last few weeks of captivity.

Clothing

In late July 1951 arrivals at Camp 1 were deloused and issued a summer uniform and in November they got their padded winter uniforms. If uniforms were ripped or torn while on a work detail they were not replaced until the next seasonal change was issued. Uniforms would frequently need cleaning from sitting in the mud listening to lectures or from chronic diarrhea. When possible they would be washed in the river or even with rain water, but no soap was available. They were dried by simply putting them back on as they had no extra clothing. This method of cleaning meant no washing during the winter.

POWs who arrived in Oct 1951 were given two uniforms, tooth powder, and soap. After a time they received a weekly ration of tobacco and sugar and the standard winter issue of uniforms. A blanket and comforter were given to every third man. It was so cold in the winter the prisoners could scrape ice from the walls of their huts.

A British reference says they slept on empty rice sacks and each squad of ten POWs received three old overcoats. Both are probably accurate, depending on the time of captivity to which they are referring.

Mail

In the spring of 1952 the prisoners were allowed to send four letters a month but whether the Chinese actually sent the letters is unclear. Some sources say the limit was one letter per month. Incoming mail began in June 1952.

When the armistice was signed fifty-five POWs were moved a few miles out of the camp towards Camp 3 where they joined about forty-five prisoners from Camp 3. They were released when the POWs from Camp 1 and 3 were released. It is unknown why this movement took place. The POWs at Camp 1 were trucked out of the camp mid-August 1953.

The Google Earth® photo above shows the village that held Camp 1 as it is today.

Camp 2

Location

Camp 2 is described in various debriefs as south, east, and north of Camp 5. The actual location of the main camp is only a few miles east of Camp 5 as the crow flies. Some POWs apparently marched directly over the mountains from Camp 5 on foot trails while others went by truck. The village names of Po-chang-ni, Chang-ni, Pi-chong-ni, and Obul are commonly found in debriefs.

The initial camp, formed in October 1951, held about 325 officers and twenty-five enlisted. The numbers included 150 US Army,

The villages that made up Camp 2 are seen above.

100 US Air Force, twenty-two US Marine Corps, ten US Navy, thirty-five British, twenty Turk, five South African, five Australian, and three Filipino. These figures include only those POWs held at Camps 2-1 and 2-2. In late October 1951 officers who had been on the Tiger Death March and then held at the Apex camps arrived at 2-1.

Camp 2 actually consisted of four separate villages in which varying numbers of POWs were held. The majority were held at the locations labeled as 2-1 and 2-2 on the maps. Camp 2-1 was the primary camp and the interrogation center for the other three. In October 1952, 2-1 was split and 2-2 formed in a village less than a mile away. Camps 2-3 and 2-4 were located in smaller, more remote villages, farther east. Camp 2-3 was where the hard core reactionary enlisted men were sent. Camp 2-4 held many POWs captured in 1952 and 1953, especially aircrew.

Camp 2-1	40-38-42N 125-31-35E	Camp 2-2	40-38-54N 125-30-59E
Camp 2-3	40-39-29N 125-41-23E	Camp 2-4	40-41-47N 125-36-16E

Description

On arrival in October 1951 the POWs were held in one large school building and a few small huts. On the accompanying maps this is labeled Camp 2-1. The large building was a former schoolhouse of wood and mud construction divided into ten rooms which held twenty-four to thirty men each. The village outside the camp area was called Pi-chong-ni. In October 1952 about half the group was moved to two newly constructed mud barracks in a village one half mile west, Camp 2-2. Company 1 remained at the original location and Company 2 went to the village down the road.   POWs were constantly separated from the main area at Camp 2 and its sub-camps and held in solitary confinement or small groups. This led to areas that were sometimes referred to as Camp 2 ½ , Camp 2 ¼ , the Annex, and No Name Valley. There were at least four areas within seven to fifteen miles of each other that were used to house the prisoners. The villages of Parun-dong and Chang-ni to the east were part of this system. Company 1 and Company 2 were at the two main locations, with Company 3 at Parun-dong, and Company 4 at Chang-ni. Annex, No Name Valley, and Camp 2 ½ apparently referred to 2-4. Camp 2 ¼ seems to have been a reference to Camp 2-3.

The first village at Camp 2, Pi-chong-ni or P'yongjang-ni, consisted of forty to fifty Korean homes. A small stream ran through the village. Until March or April of 1953 the prisoners slept on rice straw mats, twelve men on each side of the room. At that time double deck wooden bunks were built but they still had no mattresses. On their arrival at Camp 2 each individual was issued a light padded comforter, a blanket, and an overcoat. They slept shoulder to shoulder both for warmth and because of lack of space. Each squad had a bucket for water and a wash basin.

The 2-1 compound was in the eastern section of the village. It was about 80 by 110 yards, surrounded at first by one barbed wire fence and about mid 1952 by a 12' high double fence of barbed wire and saplings. These fences were separated by a three-foot space. Some sources say this double fence was not erected until the spring of 1953.

The schoolhouse building had a series of classrooms in which the POWs lived. One classroom was used as a library and stocked with numerous communist-oriented newspapers and books. The doors leading out of the building had been removed. In the hallway outside each room was a small stove used to heat water. During the last winter these stoves were moved into the rooms. Fires were allowed for at least a few hours each day. The building was set on raised ground above what had been the playground and was now the assembly area and exercise yard. Behind the school and raised even further were the huts that had been housing for the school staff. POWs living in these huts referred to the area as Snob Hill, as it was above all the other camp buildings. On the east end of the school and down a few steps was the kitchen. On the other end of the barracks was a lean-to latrine. In the village itself was a jail with barred cells used to hold POWs who had been sentenced for various "crimes."

In October of 1952 Camp 2-2 was formed just to the west of the original camp. It was in a village in a small valley just a half mile west of the main camp. The building formed a U shape. One arm was prisoner housing, the middle was the kitchen, and the other arm was a library. The prisoners slept on raised platforms in rooms with standard heated floors. In the middle of the U was their assembly area. Camp 2-2 had a wooden fence around the compound.

Camp 2-3 at Parun-dong, eight miles due east of 2-1, was established in August 1952. It held 130 to 140 enlisted ranks from other camps that the Chinese considered extremely "reactionary." They were held in about four different groups of varying sizes in and around a small village. Individual prisoners would often be forced to stand at attention, sometimes for twenty-four hours or longer, and were beaten when they would relax. Many were forced to perform hard labor. At times doors would be removed from huts and no fires allowed. It wasn't until the spring of 1953 that this kind of treatment eased up. (The British referred to camp 2-3 as Son-Yi.)

Camp 2-4 at Chang-ni (or Osang-dong or Obul), was five and a half miles northeast of 2-1. It held mostly US Air Force officers, apparently captured later in the war. Many debriefs say it was at a village of about two hundred people called Obul. The camp may have been established as early as April or May 1952. One group of 17 aircrew arrived at the end of July 1952. They were held in the standard hut with mud floors covered with old straw mats. The room was small, hot during the day and chilly at night. Each POW had a small blanket. Some were in leg irons and handcuffs. By November 1952 their numbers had risen to thirty-four and they had been moved to an old school building. The room was 20' by 30' and they slept on bamboo mats. By December, thirty more prisoners had joined the group and they had the use of a second room which they called the "rec" room/kitchen. Their compound was fenced. A prisoner who arrived at 2-4 around Thanksgiving 1952 figured about 130 POWs were held there in four separate compounds. By June 1953 the prisoners at 2-4 were divided into one group of fifty-five to seventy, one group of thirty, one group of fourteen, another of eleven, and the rest in smaller groups or in solitary confinement. Other sources say the number was closer to 200, about forty of them enlisted men. A few POWs who arrived there in late January 1953 were held in a hut outside the compound until just prior to their release in August. It was only then they were allowed to mix with their fellow POWs. In August 1953 about 130 POWs were held together in an old storage building. This was probably the bulk of POWs at Camp 2-4. The prisoners here were mostly US but included some South African, British, and Canadian. The camp was a seven mile hike from Camp 2 main. Individuals were frequently taken from Camp 2-4 back to Camp 2-1 or Pyoktong for questioning.

In all four of these camp areas were huts used to isolate those POWs, usually senior officers, who failed to demonstrate the correct attitude. Some of these huts were more like cages. POWs were kept in cells in the village jail, in woodsheds, storerooms - any isolated spot that could be found in the villages or the area around them. The senior POW was held for a year and a half in an isolated Korean house just east of Camp 2-1.

The guard population was such that there was one guard for every two POWs.

Food

At the main camp water for cooking and washing was carried by the prisoners from a stream a short distance away. Food was cooked by the POWs in the small kitchen that held nine large pots and standard Korean ovens. At mealtime each squad sent men to the kitchen to carry food back to the squad room in wooden boxes to be doled out in set amounts into the squad members' rice bowl and cup. POWs were the cooks at Camp 2-1, 2-3, and 2-4; it can be assumed that was the same for Camp 2-2. Initially they were fed two meals a day, mostly rice and soya beans. Once a week a small pig was butchered for the entire group of 370 POWs at Camp 2-1.

By the summer of 1953 the food ration differed by day of the week at Camps 2-1 and 2-2. Monday, Wednesday, and Friday they got two meals a day of rice and daikon soup (daikon is a large white radish). On Tuesday it was rice and daikon soup in the morning and rice and soya beans in the afternoon with two small buns of bread. On Saturday rice and soya beans were eaten in the afternoon but without bread. On Thursday and Sunday the meal was rice and pork soup in the morning and pork stew and bread in the afternoon. Again, pork soup meant hot water flavored with the meat of one small pig for almost 400 individuals, each of whom would receive four meals in those two days. That means one small pig provided the pork for 1600 servings. Meals were at 8:30 in the morning and 4:30 in the afternoon. What they ate depended on the season, the mood of the guards, and how well peace talks were going at Panmunjom. The closer to the end, the better they were fed. The POWs agreed the food was better than at Camp 5, but the staple was still rice and soya beans.

Every ten days the prisoners got a sugar and tobacco ration. Also issued at this time was the equivalent of about ten regular sheets of paper. Half was for rolling cigarettes and half was for toilet paper.

POWs held in solitary were fed one, two, or maybe no meals a day. That meal was commonly a watery soup of kaoling (sorghum) and a bowl of eggplant.

In December of 1952 at Camp 2-3 the food was of lesser quality than that at other camps and varied within the camp from group to group. Some were fed boiled sorghum which was frequently only half cooked and usually included lots of stones and dirt. Another source says they received one bowl of rice twice a day. That same source stated those in solitary were fed only barley, not rice. By the summer of 1953 the diet was much better, consisting of steamed rice, bread, vegetables, and sometimes meat and eggs. Sugar was also part of their ration.

At one point meals at Camp 2-4 consisted of string bean soup and rice in the morning and potatoes and rice in the evening. Every third day they got some steamed bread. One POW recorded a diet of rice, potatoes, and cabbage. Soya beans were added and in March of 1953 they were given tomato seeds to plant. A POW arriving there in May 1953 was fed twice a day on rice, corn, and beans. In August of 1953 the food improved and the meals even included hot tea. Prior to this time they usually had enough rice but it was often cold.

Medical

At 2-1 and probably 2-2 sick call was held every two days. In most cases medical care was an improvement over that provided at Camp 5 but still at minimal levels. There was a "little makeshift camp hospital" in the village about fifty yards outside the compound at 2-1. Those who caused problems for the Chinese in any of the Camp 2 compounds had medical care withheld.

At 2-1 and 2-2 the camp doctor was called "Dirty Doctor" due to his dirty hands and constant spitting on the floor. He either had little or no medical knowledge or did not want to help sick POWs. At one point a POW was used in a photo op with clean gowns, rubber gloves, and medical instruments. After the photo was taken of his supposed treatment the gowns and equipment disappeared, never to be seen again. Eventually another doctor was assigned along with some nurses. There was a dispensary at 2-3 with a POW medic who was allowed to help.

Some POWs at Camp 2-4 rated the medical treatment as good but said medical supplies were inadequate. Others said there were no medical facilities except for a "quack" who gave out pills for every medical problem. Since individuals or small groups were often held apart from other POWs and placed in categories according to their "behavior," both statements are probably accurate. There were only two deaths at the Camp 2 compounds and they were accidental.

Daily Activities

Initially the prisoners at Camp 2-1 dug latrines and food pits and carried rocks to build areas in the camp. They hauled wood and water as in other camps. In the summer of 1952 they helped build Camp 2-2. It was common for a group to be marched to the Yalu to unload barges and sometimes allowed to swim .

In the first months at Camp 2-1 the POWs would be roused at dawn each day for roll-call and some type of exercise in the assembly area. They would return to their quarters where the squad leaders had to read out loud for an hour from Communist material. Breakfast was at 8:30 followed by two hours of lecture with a guard in the room. After a break they would have more political study from two until four. At 4:30 they received their evening meal followed by more political study in small groups. Every evening the entire camp was assembled to hear a speech by the camp commander. Even in the winter this all took place in unheated rooms or in the outdoor assembly area. Guards were present and the prisoners were made to sit still and "not make the jokes or rude noises." In the fall of 1951 there were nine and a half hours of lectures and study each day. By April of 1952 this had been cut down to about four hours a day. After April 1952 the lecture/study program ceased.

After the group lectures were ended the prisoners were allowed to play baseball, volleyball, and soccer. Camp 2-4 was supplied with reading material, which was generally Communist books and newspapers. They were also issued playing cards. Some played chess with home-made pieces. In the late fall of 1952, Camp 2-3 was allowed to construct a small bathhouse for their own use. Basketball and volleyball equipment were provided.

Around Easter of 1953 some POWs from Camp 2-3 were allowed to visit 2-1 and 2-2 for brief sports competitions in softball, basketball, volleyball, and soccer. By the time of the first prisoner exchange in 1953, prisoners at Camp 2-1 were allowed to listen to English news broadcasts from Peking. Just before the final release they were given Red Cross supplies.

Treatment

Use of "the hole" and extended periods of solitary confinement were common in all the Camp 2 villages. Senior officers were punished for trying to maintain military order. The three harshest sentences to solitary confinement stretched for four months, one year, and eighteen months. These sentences were for the three senior officers in the camp. One of the charges against them was their failure to send Christmas greetings to the camp commander, Ding, and the general leading Chinese forces in Korea. The "hole" could be anything from a single hut, a jail cell in a local police station, a storage shed, or an outhouse, to an actual hole in the ground covered with a door. At Camp 2-1 one of the holes used was a rat-infested latrine in the village, still used by the villagers. Individuals were kept under the latrine for as many as two weeks at a time, even in the winter. There were POWs held in these various locations who were never allowed contact with other prisoners. In August and September of 1952 prisoners from 2-1 who were held in actual cells in the village jail noticed POWs they did not recognize being held in a hole covered with logs. The men were kept in this hole one at a time and then disappeared. A few weeks later the hole was filled in and the mystery POWs never seen again. Debriefs of POWs held at Camp 2-4 tell of being sent to main Camp 2-1 in September 1952 for interrogation. They were held in pits dug in the ground in the village near the POW compound. The holes were about 5' wide and 6' high. There was a wooden door with logs piled over it. Food was simply passed to them through the door. Once the interrogations were finished they were sent back to 2-4.

Treatment at the four camps varied depending on the alleged offense. When held in the jail cells in the town, a prisoner was expected to sit on the ground in the middle of the cell all day. Depending on the guard, this rule was enforced with beatings. One prisoner was stripped naked and forced to stand at attention for twenty-four hours. His legs were beat with an ax handle when he wavered. Others had food and water withheld for five or six days. Some were strung up by their hands or feet. Some were placed before firing squads. Another was tied to a telephone pole during a February night wearing only a cotton shirt and pants. Soon after this he signed a confession. Another POW was tied to an overhead beam from his wrists which were tied behind his back. The rope was then pulled tight so he had to stand on his tiptoes. He was kept in this position all night. The next day he was stripped to his waist and made to stand outside for the entire December day. That night he was tied to the beam again. Two POWs were confined to a small stone hut at one of the camps for one month. The floor had been flooded and was solid ice.

In February 1953 a POW was sentenced to seventy-seven days solitary confinement for not cooperating properly. He was placed in a store room in a Korean hut with two blankets. The temperature would drop as low as thirty degrees below zero during which time he slept on the dirt floor.

Another prisoner was placed in the hole from the first week of April 1953 to that July. During that time he was deprived of bathing, exercise, medical care, and light. He was constantly threatened by the guards pointing their weapons at him and pulling the trigger.

In September of 1952 a POW at 2-1 was placed in a hole of five square feet for six days. Once a day a bowl of rice and maybe some bread was passed through the door. He was then taken out for questioning. When he gave no answers he was placed back in the hole for two more days. The above are only examples of treatment endured by so many.

Prisoners would be sentenced to the hole for talking back to the guards or even for singing. One was charged with attempting to convince a fellow POW to sleep past morning wake-up. Any show of leadership would get a POW "arrested," "tried," and "sentenced" to a period of time in isolation. At one "trial," after the charges were read, the "court" adjourned for approximately three minutes. On returning to the room the sentences were read – from a typed sheet which had been on the table all the while the "court" had been in adjournment to determine those sentences. The more serious offenses meant being confined in very small spaces.

Prisoners being punished for various offenses were grouped in five classes. First class meant time in jail in groups of no more than thirty and no contact with POWs outside the group. They were given sugar, tobacco, and soup. Second class meant you were held in groups of four or less and you received occasional sugar and tobacco. Third class were given no sugar, tobacco, or soup and only allowed to bathe occasionally. Fourth class were held in solitary in a house or shed. There was no sugar, tobacco, soup, or washing. Fifth class were held in solitary in a place that was both physically and mentally uncomfortable. The POW was cold, cramped, and received no food. At times confinement to the hole meant using your cell as your latrine. Many of the prisoners who were put in these classifications were pilots who would not admit to germ warfare. Those who attempted escapes were usually punished by solitary confinement. A version of this method of assigning offenses by class seemed to exist in some or all of the other camps along the Yalu as well.

Prisoners were constantly pulled from the group, frequently at night, for extensive questioning about alleged offenses. Written confessions were demanded and often dictated. POWs had to guess how long they could refuse to sign these statements before they were thrown into solitary confinement. Crossing a very fine line led to harsh treatment.

In 1952 there were forty-one escapes from Camp 2-1 (Camp 2-2 is probably included in this figure). Some of the escapees managed to stay free for a few days; others were caught in the act. When drying cabbage leaves on the roof of the schoolhouse the prisoners would spell out P O W in an attempt to signal friendly aircraft. They would even stamp out P O W in the snow. Just as in the escape attempts, they were always caught and someone spent time in solitary for their efforts. Around Easter of 1953 at least three POWs escaped from Camp 2-4 and were caught that same day. Various debriefs say a POW was killed during this attempt. Some say he was an American and others say he was British but that name appears on listings of British survivors. It may well be there was no death. One prisoner was wounded in an escape attempt from Camp 2-3.

At Camp 2-3 the prisoners received Chinese uniforms including the standard rubber/canvas tennis shoes which were not adequate protection for the winter temperatures. They were fed one bowl of rice twice a day and went each day into the woods to gather firewood. The majority of POWs here tended to be left alone by the Chinese. An American was put in charge of cooking. A small bathhouse was built using a fifty-five gallon drum to heat water for bathing Japanese style. By spring of 1953 food for most of the prisoners was greatly improved, as it was at most camps.

A small group of about fifteen hard-core reactionaries was first held in a separate building about one hundred yards from the bulk of the men at Camp 2-3. The only door was kept locked at all times by the guards. Permission had to be granted even to use the latrine. In April of 1953 this group was moved to another building which was surrounded by a 10' high brush fence. They were allowed to move in and out of this house at will, but had to remain inside the fence. A sentry box, manned twenty-four hours a day, stood at the only opening in the fence. After the move to this location, they received a tobacco ration and were given books to read. In general this group was treated much more harshly than others in the camp. In February they spent two weeks with their firewood supply cut off. This was a throwback to the treatment during the first winter of 1950-51 when most of the POW deaths occurred.

Any perceived misbehavior led to a beating or solitary confinement. A bucket of sorghum was brought to them twice a day. If the guard commander was in a good mood they got rice for one of the daily meals. Anything to sour his mood meant only sorghum for the prisoners, so they ate sorghum for weeks at a stretch. After the move in April 1953 they received the same meals as the rest of the camp, as well as new uniforms, soap, and razors, and were allowed to bathe in the river. However, they remained isolated from others in the camp.

Clothing

Standard summer and winter issue. Prisoners were also issued a blanket, a light cotton comforter, and an overcoat. In December of 1951 each POW at Camp 2-1 was issued a heavy blanket and a padded winter uniform. Periodically there were issues of underwear, towels, and soap.

Mail

Prisoners were allowed to write letters. Whether they received any depended partly on their compliance with camp regulations and their attitude toward the guards. The common excuse for no mail arriving in camp was that US planes were constantly bombing supply routes. At one point at Camp 2-1 they were shown mostly burned envelopes as proof. On further investigation the POWs noted that some of the letters were ones they had written the day before. One POW received one letter fourteen months after he was captured. His family had sent over 300 letters to him during the same time period. By January 1953 mail at 2-1 was delivered every two or three weeks. Some got mail from home; others did not.

The prisoners held in isolation at 2-3 were finally allowed to send letters home in April of 1953.

Release

The first POWs left the main camp at 2-1 on 5 August 1953 with the last group leaving on 19 August. They traveled by truck to Manpo

and then south by train. Even at the end, the Chinese were trying to
get signed confessions from POWs still held in isolation with threats
they would be left behind. In May and June 1953 Camp 2-3 was broken up and the POWs sent to the various enlisted camps. The group of
hard-core reactionaries held separately were sent to Camp 2-4 in May
and held there until late June. At Camp 2-4 they were still held separately at a farm house a few hundred yards from the main POW area.
A machine-gun was set up to cover the house. After six weeks they
were sent, a few at a time, to Camps 1, 3, or 5 to be released after the
Armistice.

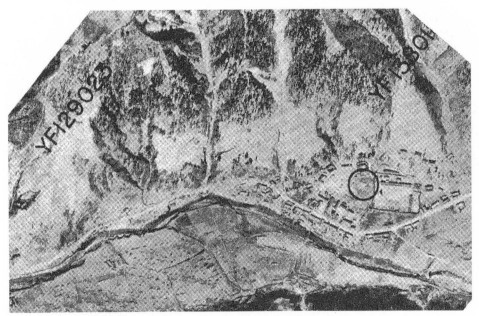

*The US Air Force photo above shows Camp 2 Company 1 in 1953. The long
school building/barracks, the exercise yard, and the fence surrounding them
can be seen next to the circle marking Camp 2.*

The *2010 Google Earth® picture clearly shows the same building and exercise yard more than fifty years later.*

In the Google Earth® photo above Camp 3 south denotes the area holding the POWs from Camp 5 who arrived in August 1951 along with the Tiger Death March survivors after their arrival in October 1951. The Chinese Headquarters area was in the middle. Camp 3 north held the October 1951 arrivals from Kang-dong and the group from Camp 5 that arrived in March 1952.

Camp 3

Location: Southern 40-31-32N 125-10-15E
Northern 40-32-17N 125-10-58 E

Camp 3 was about fourteen miles (as the crow flies) southwest of Camp 5 at Pyoktong. It was located on two points of land about a mile and a half apart on the eastern side of an estuary of the Yalu approximately six miles south of the Yalu itself. As with Camp 1 the names Changsong and Chongsong are used in relation to Camp 3.

Description

Camp 3 was first established in July or August of 1951 with the arrival of about 150 POWs sent from Camp 5 on three barges. This group moved into three large buildings and proceeded to build the camp on the southern, or lower, point. In early October a group from Kangdong arrived and were housed at the northern point. In late October the survivors of the Tiger Death March were brought down from Camp 7 (part of the Apex Camps). This group was moved into Korean homes in the village at the southern point. The NCOs within the Tiger group were separated for a few days and then housed with the rest of the Tigers. The recollection of these men is that the Tiger NCOs were never sent to Camp 4, but stayed at the southern point of Camp 3. The day before the Tiger survivors came into camp a second group arrived from Camp 5. (This may have been the group from Kangdong or two trucks that each carried eight POWs from Camp 5.) They were held in the northernmost compound, about a mile north of the camp headquarters. Some time in the spring of 1952 some prisoners from the Kangdong group, labelled as troublemakers, were moved down next to the Tigers. In March of 1953 a group of thirty to forty POWs was marched from Camp 5 to Camp 3. They were told they were "a distraction" to the Chinese efforts at Camp 5. It appears they were also placed on the northern point. For one day in the spring or summer of 1952 the prisoners at the northern point were marched down to the southern point for athletic games with their fellow POWs. Other than that the two groups were kept apart.

In October of 1951 all officers were sent to Camp 2. In August of

1952 all NCOs were sent to Camp 4; the British prisoners were sent to Camp 1; and American black enlisted were sent to Camp 5. After these transfers, Camp 3 held only white American privates and corporals.

Again, the Tigers say their NCOs were kept at Camp 3 and not sent to Camp 4. The Tigers were kept separate from the rest of Camp 3 and some POWs considered troublemakers from the northern part of Camp 3 were sent down to live with or near the Tigers.

In the fall of 1951 the POWs on the southern point began construction on four or five buildings about sixty feet long and thirty feet wide. The walls were mud and the roofs were straw. Some POWs were moved into them in March of 1952. Each building housed about seventy-five men. Charcoal was provided as a fuel for heat. On or about Easter 1953 one of these larger barracks fell down. Men in that company refused to stay in any of the remaining buildings. The entire company was then moved to the northern compound. In the spring of 1952 bunks were built for at least some of the prisoners on the northern point. Some recall being moved from these buildings in the fall of 1952 into Korean houses as they were easier to keep heated during the winter.

Some refer to Camp 3 as a reactionary camp or a hard labor camp for reactionaries. This may be so, but whole companies from other camps were initially transferred here, not individuals or small groups. There was the small group sent from Camp 5 in March of 1953. They apparently were a "distraction" and that certainly meant reactionary to the Chinese. There was a separate Reactionary Squad set up at Camp 3. Those POWs that continuously frustrated the Chinese efforts at "re-education" were put into this squad, which at one point included about fifteen men. At night they would sneak out on the road running through the camp and plant nails to flatten tires on trucks carrying Chinese troops and supplies. When they continued to harass the progressives in camp they were put in a building apart from the company area. Finally, in September of 1952, some from this squad were transferred to Camp 2-3. In addition, another group of POWs was removed from their companies in the spring and summer of 1952 and kept near the camp headquarters. Some of them were also transferred to Camp 2-3.

Those POWs from these two groups not sent to Camp 2-3 were sent to join the Tiger group at the southern point. (The two groups mentioned here may have actually been just one group.) All of these men were considered troublemakers by the Chinese. Camp 2-3 was definitely a camp set up specifically for reactionaries.

For some reason, at the end of June 1953, about fifty-five POWs from Camp 3 were sent by truck to a location between Camp 3 and Camp 1. Most of them were housed in two long buildings while some slept under the roofs of open cattle sheds. They were joined by about forty-five prisoners sent from Camp 1. Their only work details were to carry firewood and collect their rations from the distribution point. There was no mistreatment and they were released about 15 August when Camp 1 and Camp 3 were released.

There are references to a separate camp set up between Camp 3 and Camp 5 in May or June 1953, referred to as 3rd Company Camp 3 or Camp 3, Branch 2. It is most likely there was no such camp but instead confusion brought on by the fact an entire company was moved from the southern point to the northern point at Easter 1953 and/or the movement of the fifty-five POWs from Camp 3 to near Camp 1 at the end of June 1953.

There were escape attempts made at Camp 3. These men were always sentenced to hard labor of some kind.

Food

For the September 1951 arrivals, meals were rice and pumpkin broth for about a week. Then meals were rice or sorghum, changing after time to rice and sorghum mixed. In the spring of 1952, vegetables were added to the diet. A December 1952 arrival said the diet was sorghum and millet with very little rice. The food was commonly filled with worms and bugs. Those prisoners from Camp 5 said the food at Camp 3 was better.

Two meals a day was the norm. In the summer they would usually receive a piece of bread for a snack at noon. Turnips were stored in large root cellars dug by the POWs. This allowed servings of turnip soup during the winter which cured the night blindness experienced by both the prisoners and their guards.

Medical

Initially, little if any medical care was provided. Prisoners who were considered ill were sent to the "hospital" at Camp 1. At least one source mentions a dispensary within Camp 3 to which he was sent for a minor injury. Others mention sick call being held once a week. By the spring of 1952 food and medical treatment had improved, as they had at most camps by then. At least one POW was sent to a hospital at Camp 3, then to the hospital at Camp 5, and finally back to Camp 3. Little medical treatment was given, but he did receive a bath, better food, some vitamins, a blanket, and allowed to sleep as much as possible.

Daily Activities

The first arrivals were used to construct the buildings and roads of the camp itself. After that, details consisted of moving dirt and rocks and going into the mountains for firewood. Swimming was eventually allowed and a volleyball area was set up and equipment provided, probably in the summer of 1952. In the fall of 1951 Communist newspapers were provided for reading material. Until April 1952 the POWs received daily political lectures. In the spring of 1952 some, if not all, of the POWs at the northern point were marched down to the southern point for one day of athletic competition with the POWs there.

Treatment

Prisoners were often sent to what they called "regiment." This was the Chinese headquarters area between the northern and southern compound. At regiment they would be questioned or punished. Solitary confinement was used at Camp 3 as elsewhere. During this time an individual would be held in a small area with very little light allowed in. For the entire day they would have to sit cross-legged with their back straight. Guards would check several times an hour and jab the prisoner with a pole or bayonet if they were not sitting up. One prisoner spent six weeks this way. Some had their hands handcuffed or tied behind their backs twenty-four hours a day. That meant eating off the floor like a dog and defecating in their pants. Some POWs were suspended from the wall with a rope tied to their toes and their hands tied behind their back. Breaking of minor rules led to confinement or withholding of food and soap. The progress of peace talks determined how quick the guards were to beat prisoners for breaking rules. Normal rations of food, soap, and tobacco were reduced for individuals who displayed "hostile attitudes." Displeasing your host meant you needed help adjusting your attitude. A week in the hole without blankets or heat and little food usually helped with that adjustment. One POW was held in a 4' by 8' room from November 1952 until March 1953, allowed out only for interrogation. Beatings could be severe. Prisoners would be returned to their company area with obvious cuts and bruises.

There are reports that when the POWs at Camp 3 refused to sign a peace appeal, the last prisoner in line was hung. The prisoners in camp were then told they would get the same if they did not sign. There were prisoners in other camps that were hung by having their hands and feet tied to a cross for various periods of time. Whether the reference here is to the same treatment or actually being hung by the neck is not clear.

For at least a short time POWs had an exercise period each morning in which they were marched down the road and double-timed back.

As usual, prisoners were not allowed to have much contact with other prisoners outside their company.

Clothing

POWs who arrived at Camp 3 in the fall of 1951 were given the standard Chinese cotton padded uniform to replace the uniforms they had been wearing since capture. This included Chinese horsehair padded tennis shoes. They were issued one blanket and one quilt per person. Anything left of their original uniforms had to be turned in when the Chinese uniforms were issued. The summer clothing issue consisted of two pair of tennis shoes, two cotton uniforms, a cap, cotton gloves, undershorts and shirts.

Mail

POWs were given their first mail from home in January 1952.

Release

At release in August 1953 Camp 3 held about 850 POWs. About 12 August the prisoners were told the Red Cross was coming into the camp. They cleaned up the camp and were given new uniforms. On the day the Red Cross arrived tables were set up and beer, jam, fish, and chicken were placed on the tables. As the Red Cross jeeps came into camp the prisoners were ordered to sit at the tables.

Exactly who was in Camp 3, when they were there, and in what part of the camp they were held would seem to be a complicated issue. The information above is taken from individual POW debriefs recorded in 1953 and personal recollections provided to the author in 2010.

Camp 4

Location: 40-54N 126-02E

Camp 4 was established in August 1952 when NCOs held in the various camps were sent north to where the Wiwon Gang River enters the Yalu. At that time it became the northernmost POW camp in North Korea. The Apex camps had been farther north but were closed down in October 1951. There were a few NCOs held at Camps 2-3 and 2-4 and the Tiger NCOs were at Camp 3.

Description

About 400 NCOs were sent here by barge from Camp 5 on 14 August 1952. They left about 9:30 am and arrived at midnight that day. Others came by truck from Camps 1 and 3 on 15 August. One report says the village at Wiwon consisted of about 600 buildings. Others refer to the village of Kuuptong. No village exists there today because of an increase in the water level. Some POWs were initially held in an old schoolhouse, others in old barracks buildings. Eventually the camp held about 600 POWs. They were divided into three companies. Companies One and Two were on the north side of the river and Company Three was on the south. Each company area was surrounded by barbed wire. A rock wall separated Companies One and Two.

The majority of POWs were American. Less than fifty were British; twenty-five were Turkish; twelve Filipino, a few French, and one Japanese civilian. Company One held most of the non-American POWs and about 200 Americans. Company Two consisted of about 200 Americans. The sixty African-American sergeants were in Company Three along with about 100 other Americans, the Filipinos and the Japanese.

Food

The diet at Camp 4 was more or less the same as they had experienced at other camps at that time.   Meals were corn or rice with a small cube of meat every few days. As usual, when the peace talks were going well they ate better. After the Armistice was signed the POWs received one can of pre-cooked beef or pork per day for every two men in addition to the normal meals.

Treatment

One of the first tasks of the POWs at Camp 4 was to build the rock wall between Companies One and Two. Prisoners then worked pulling grass, carrying logs for fuel, digging ditches, and building roads and bridges. One POW estimated the round trip to gather fuel wood was a twelve mile hike. The wood detail meant going into the woods with sleds to haul back the firewood.

Initially they slept on the floor like elsewhere. Around Thanksgiving 1952 bunks or Japanese-style sleeping platforms were built. Some form of electric lights was installed in the barracks. The standard summer and winter uniforms were issued. Brick stoves were installed in the barracks. Individuals were issued a blanket and a comforter, commonly sewing the two together to form a sleeping bag.

In November of 1952 about 50 POWs from Camp 4 were allowed to participate in the "Olympics" held at Camp 5, an event lasting about two weeks. They traveled by barge down to Camp 5 and by truck back north to Camp 4 when the event was over.

There were limited attempts at indoctrination. For the most part that meant having to read Communist newspapers. That winter and spring they were given lectures on bacteriological warfare. Loud speakers broadcast the latest propaganda throughout the camp.

There were escape attempts at Camp 4. These POWs were held for various amounts of time in solitary confinement. One punishment for being uncooperative was to strip a prisoner, hang him from a beam by two ropes tied to his wrists, then a third and shorter rope running from the beam to his penis. He had to keep himself pulled up off the floor by the ropes on his wrists. Another punishment was to be thrown into a root cellar, the prisoners's hands tied behind his back. In the cold of winter no blankets would be provided and in the summer the heat would be suffocating.

Medical

Medical care here was somewhat of an improvement for those arriving from Camp 1. Unsanitary conditions created a fly problem. At one point prisoners were given one cigarette per day if they killed 200 flies. They would pool their dead flies and allow different men in the squad to earn the cigarette each day. Medical treatment was minimal.

Mail

The prisoners were told they had to write "Against American Aggression" on their envelopes home. Rather than send letters home with that statement many never wrote at all.

Release

The entire camp left about 20 August 1953 by truck for Manpo. A washed-out road caused them to sleep in the trucks one night and then walk the last few miles into Manpo.

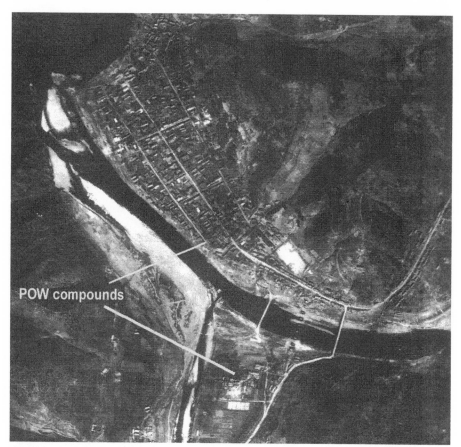

POW compounds

Camp 4 in 1953. Changes in the river level have completely flooded the area since then. NARA photo.

Camp 5 at Pyoktong as it is seen on Google Earth® today.

Camp 5

Location: 40 37 35 N 125 25 49 E

Camp 5 was in the town of Pyoktong on the end of a peninsula in a backwater area of the Yalu river. Pyoktong was a former Japanese resort town of 400 to 500 homes. The peninsula pointed west towards the Yalu with water to the north and south. This was the first permanent camp and the only one until March 1951 when Camp 1 was opened. After March 1952 no new POWs came into Camp 5.

Description

The first group of American POWs arrived at Pyoktong on or about 20 November 1950. The village was hit shortly before or shortly after their arrival by B-29s and the prisoners were moved a few miles away to the southeast to what became known as the Valley. They remained there until 18 January 1951 when they were returned to Pyoktong. In another debrief the individual says he arrived at Pyoktong on 25 November and remained for two days before being sent to the Valley. In the beginning at Pyoktong the POWs were housed in the standard Korean homes in the bombed-out section of the town. They slept on the bare floor, had no blankets, and were allowed no fires. One POW recalls having a fire part of the day three days out of the week in that first winter. Initially they slept twenty-five individuals in a room. By the fall of 1951 the number per room was down to about ten. Half the POW population had died and some of the living were sent to Camp 3. Doors were put on the huts and gauze sheeting was used on the windows to keep out flies. The issue of whether fires were allowed in the huts remains unclear. POW debriefs vary as to when they had fires in their huts. Some say very little heat was available in the huts and some huts had none at all that first winter. Other debriefs say no fires allowed the first winter, no fires until March or April 1951, and no heat at all until the last winter. The reality would seem to be that the prisoner huts were seldom heated by anything other than body heat that first winter.

In his book, *Reactionary*, Lloyd W. Pate recalls his arrival at Camp 5 early in March of 1951. From the top of the hill to the east of the camp it "looked like heaven." They saw houses with stacks of wood outside which would keep them warm. They did not know many of the houses lacked doors or windows. As they got closer they saw the stacks of wood were actually bodies of dead POWs. "Heaven" became hell.

As at all the camps, the POWs were separated by race and rank. Camp 5 started with five companies. One company held all the black or Spanish-speaking Americans and other enlisted UN troops. One held white American and British enlisted, another white American and Turkish enlisted. Non-commissioned officers and officers were in separate compounds. Various re-arrangements of this system were used over the next two years.

Initially the only water source was in the enlisted compound. Ice covered the interior walls of their huts. The POWs were lice-infested and most had severe diarrhea or dysentery. The latrines were inadequate in size and number and poorly located. They were frequently near the company kitchens and some were too close to the only well. This meant feces was everywhere-on their clothing, in the huts, and all around their compounds. The only clothing they had was what was left from their time of capture. POWs arriving in March 1951 found men in tattered uniforms, many with no shoes. Dead bodies were stacked outside the huts awaiting burial.

Food

In the beginning the POWs were generally fed twice a day. The meals were usually wormy corn. In the early months of 1951 rice rarely appeared. Each prisoner received about a tea cup full of the boiled grain per meal, often undercooked. Very small amounts of beans or turnips sometimes accompanied the grain. As time went on one meal a week would be rice. By that summer sorghum replaced the corn and some kind of vegetable became more common. Meat was very rare and almost no salt was added to their diet. A British diary said that in March of 1951 the daily food intake was 200 grams per day. As soon as plants appeared in the spring, the POWs would pick any they could find to add some kind of greens to their diet.

Prior to May 1951 all meals consisted of cracked corn or barley.

There was no salt and no bread. The leftover barley coffee was used to wash their makeshift bowls. By the fall of 1951 each company had its own kitchen with POW cooks boiling the food in large pots. By this time the Chinese had made an obvious decision to improve conditions enough to keep their entire population of POWs from dying. Clean water was piped in. The food improved to where they were getting more rice and sometimes a little meat in the rice. Every six weeks a small pig was butchered for each company. The prisoners had learned they could not drink cold water from wells or streams; they boiled it first and drank it warm or made some kind of coffee. After November 1951 each prisoner usually received part of a canteen cup of sugar every ten days. This was frequently used by the cooks to enhance a meal or two for all. By this time each POW had been issued two small tin bowls, a cup, and a spoon. One member of the squad would pick up the chow box and soup bucket from the company kitchen and take it to the squad hut. The bowls would be set out and food distributed evenly. Leftovers were then given to the next few men and a record kept of where they left off. At the next meal, leftovers would pick up where they left off the previous meal.

In January 1952 they started receiving rice and turnip broth daily and sometimes steamed bread. By July soy beans and fish started appearing. From August 1952 on, the food gradually increased in amount so that the quantity became sufficient but the quality was still poor. The POWs were able to keep track of how peace talks were going at Panmunjom as the quality and quantity of the daily meals went up or down accordingly. Food was also used as the "carrot on the end of the stick" in Chinese efforts to get individuals or the entire camp population to sign confessions or peace petitions. Prisoners who did not "demonstrate the correct attitude" had their food withheld.

Medical

Almost none of the wounded had received any medical treatment prior to arrival at Camp 5 and for months next to none was provided there. No one had been able to bathe since their capture and no bathing was made possible at Camp 5 until the winter ice melted from the estuary in April or May of 1951. Prisoners weren't able to shave or cut their hair. Everyone was infested with lice. Dysentery, pneumonia, and malnutrition were rampant. The dead were frequently stripped by POWs who needed the clothing and the bodies then stacked outside the huts until collection by the burial detail. No clothing was issued by the Chinese that first winter but those POWs who came from Death Valley had been issued a coat, blanket, and hat.

The death rate at Camp 5 was horrendous. It can best be understood by looking at a peace petition the Chinese forced everyone to sign in June of 1951 that had 1671 signatures. Five months earlier there had been about 3500 men in the camp. One POW recorded over seventy bodies carried out of camp in one day that first winter.

Initially there was no hospital at Camp 5; instead there was a "dispensary" in the various company areas. One POW doctor was allowed to hold sick call but could only suggest to the Chinese that some individuals were too ill to work. His supplies were little more than aspirin and recycled bandages. In January 1951 one company dispensary was described as a dirty shack with a paper-covered door. It was common for "patients" to freeze to death during the night. In May of 1951 a sick company was created and the dispensaries closed down. Most of the sick were kept in the sick company and not sent to the central hospital. The POW doctor had about ten medics to help with a patient load of about 100 men. Infected wounds were best treated by letting maggots clean out the dead tissue. In July 1951 the POW doctor was removed from the enlisted compound. Earlier a central hospital was established in a Buddhist monastery on the hill in the town east of the POW area. A prisoner who arrived at Camp 5 in May 1951 was put directly in this hospital. There were over 100 POWs lying on the floor, covered in lice and feces. They were not bathed and received no medication. The dead were left with the living for days. The injections commonly given patients caused many to die soon after. The very ill were frequently put in a hut at the rear of the hospital and left on their own to die.

Patients in the hospital were fed slightly better than other POWs and that was the best medicine they received. Still, the death rate averaged twenty per day in the hospital itself. The POW doctors that worked there were not allowed to list malnutrition as a cause of death.

The Chinese camp commander finally told the doctors the deaths must cease. More medicine was made available, but the better diet for the POWs was the major factor in improving their overall health.

By August 1951 conditions improved. A Chinese medical team was brought in, DDT was used, and the food improved. During the last two weeks of August no deaths occurred in the hospital. There were no deaths at all in the officers' compound after August. A senior Chinese officer told the POW doctors there had been no deaths in any of the camps that September. In September most patients in the hospital were sent back to their company area. Medical charts were drawn up on each of the forty patients who remained and they were finally treated like real patients in a real hospital. The Chinese medical team seemed to be there only to improve the health of those forty patients. Their condition improved to bring them to the best health since their capture. At that point the medical team began a series of injections that lasted for two weeks. Then each patient underwent a procedure in which a chicken liver was surgically inserted in the side of the chest. They were told this was a new Russian procedure which would cure all diseases from pneumonia to syphilis. They were monitored for another month and then returned to their company areas. On return, they found that while they had been receiving almost excellent medical care at the hospital, medical issues in the companies were still going untreated. Few of the forty had any reaction to the chicken liver, positive or negative. There are references to this procedure being conducted in other camps but these are most likely not valid. Those references provide no details and seem to be based on second hand stories where a POW simply assumes the events happened in his camp.

A POW who arrived from Mining Camp in late October 1951 was placed directly in the main hospital for beri beri, dysentery, and malnutrition. For the next two months he and the fifty-four patients with him were given a better diet which included small amounts of fish or pork and apples. They were allowed to rest and given vitamin injections. He was released into a company in the camp on 1 January 1952. Even with the improved care and diet, twelve of the fifty-five died.

By August 1952 medical treatment improved but never became adequate. In the fall of 1952 many had dysentery again, some having

twenty or more bowel movements a day. Night blindness returned due
to a lack of vitamins. This lack of vitamins also exaggerated any common medical problem such as an earache or toothache. For their entire
time at Camp 5 prisoners had to deal with lice during the winter and
bed bugs, fleas, and flies in the summer.

Daily Activities

After the first winter a day at Camp 5 would start with a bell at
5:00 am to announce roll call and group exercise. Morning chow was
about 8:30. Lectures went on during the day with some time for company details such as sweeping up the squad area, picking up chow,
gathering firewood, and carrying water. About 4:30 pm another bell
would announce evening chow to be followed by speeches. The bell
at 9:00 pm was the signal everyone had to be in their huts to be
counted again. During winter months the day would start at 7:00 am.
By 1952 there was only one roll call at the end of the day. This schedule varied slightly depending on the season. The prisoners were only
fed twice a day, except for the summer months when some kind of
light snack like peanuts, was distributed at noon. Once the efforts at
"re-education" ended in 1952, the majority of the day was free time
except for the work details mentioned above. Chinese music and
slanted English news were broadcast over loudspeakers around the
camp.

In the spring of 1951 work assigned to the prisoners at Camp 5
consisted of cleaning up camp, digging air raid shelters, and unload-
ing barges. During the last two winters they would cross the ice-cov-
ered estuary to gather firewood. Many POWs thought they were
crossing the Yalu when they crossed the ice to bury their dead or
gather firewood. This was not the case as the camp was not directly
on the Yalu.

By the summer of 1952 sports equipment was supplied. Swimming was allowed at midday. Some prisoners put together a band
using home-made instruments. A group of British POWs put on
plays. The Chinese would periodically show a propaganda movie.
A library was set up with mostly Communist oriented books, maga-
zines, and newspapers. The reading material was in English and some

well known novels were included. During the last year prisoners spent lots of time playing cards and talking with fellow prisoners in their company. Since no new POWs were brought into Camp 5 after the spring of 1952 the newspapers were read carefully to try and determine the real progress of the war. In August all the NCOs were moved north to Camp 4. The camp still had five companies: US white POWs, US black POWs, the Turks, the English, and one for other nationalities. Some English POWs were transferred in from Camp 3. In the winter of 1952-53 electric lights were installed in at least one building for the prisoners to play cards, chess, and ping pong.

In November of 1952 an inter-camp Olympics was held at Camp 5. Teams from most of the other camps were brought in between the

Chinese photo of POWs at the end of the November 1952 "Olympics" held at Camp 5. The mountainside in the background gives an idea of why it was so difficult to escape. All the camps were surrounded by these mountains.

14th and 26th of November to participate. The Chinese used this event to show pictures to the world of the happy prisoners enjoying their lenient treatment. The POWs used this event as an opportunity to visit each other, get news on the war and events back home from recent captures, and to compile more complete lists of captures and deaths.

Early in 1953 there was a fly killing campaign with cigarette "rewards" for a certain number of flies presented. This actually reduced the number of flies, but the open latrines were the real problem. By this time in the camps boredom was a problem, so even a fly killing campaign was welcome. In March, material was provided to make bunk beds with ropes woven back and forth to create a mattress.

Treatment

The first prisoners into Camp 5 came from The Valley and Death Valley and were in terrible condition. Nothing changed once they arrived in late January 1951. As soon as they arrived they were divided into separate compounds, as the Chinese were determined to prevent any military discipline on the part of the American POWs. They were herded into bare rooms of the mud Korean homes, as many as twenty-five per room. They slept on the floor with only their clothing and body heat to keep them warm. Ice covered the walls and feces the floors. No one had been able to bathe since their capture. Wounds were untreated. The dying that had begun in the temporary camps and on the marches continued. Their food intake was so minimal some prisoners would paw through fresh feces looking for undigested beans or kernels of corn. The overall scene was reminiscent of the concentration camps of World War II.

During the months of February and March 1951 the only activity required of the POWs was to help bury the dead. That meant collecting the bodies stacked outside the huts and carrying them across the estuary to Boot Hill. There they would use their hands to scrape into the snow as much as possible and place the bodies. The effort required to do this meant some prisoners died while carrying their dead comrades to this make-shift burial ground and were themselves left on Boot Hill.

In these first months the prisoners learned life could actually get worse. Men were commonly thrown into a variation of "the hole." In one case this was a concrete cell. Other variations were covered-over storage pits dug into the ground, cages dug into the side of a hill, or isolated huts away from the prisoner compound. Being put in the hole sometimes meant a loss of two or three days' meals and exposure to the cold with no protection other than what they were wearing. A common punishment was to force a prisoner to stand at attention outside in the cold. When they relaxed they were beaten with fists or rifle butts. This sometimes went on all day and into the night. Others were hung from rafters by their wrists for extended periods of time. For some this meant months of not being able to use their hands, in one case more than a year. More than a few were hung by their wrists in full view of the entire camp. After an escape attempt in March a POW was beaten and put in the hole for three days. Then his body was removed and buried. Another escape attempt led to the prisoner being tied up outside in below- zero temperatures and water thrown on him until he died. In the summer the hole might be a shack or a cage dug into the side of a hill. All light would be blocked to increase the heat, and food and water withheld. It was not just escape attempts or theft of food that earned prisoners time in the hole. Any display of an "improper attitude" could also put them there.

Rank provided no exemption to this treatment: enlisted and officer alike were beaten or thrown in the hole. One senior officer made a remark the Chinese did not like. For that remark he was beaten and tortured for three weeks, much of that time being hung by his wrists. When he finally signed a confession of his "crimes," he was returned to the compound. He told his fellow officers he was supposed to inform on them to the Chinese. He died a few weeks later. An officer who attempted escape was tied up and paraded through the camp. A rope around his neck was yanked to cause choking. He was then thrown in the hole and fed cold grain twice a day. After a month he finally signed a confession and was released from the hole. It was months before he could use his hands. With a starvation diet and lack of medical care a beating or confinement in the hole frequently pushed the body beyond its limit and death followed. This really meant the mood of the guards could determine whether a POW lived or died, as time in the hole or standing at attention in the cold all day was often enough to tip an individual to the point of not being able to recover.

In April 1951 the lectures began. The entire camp was told they were guilty of war crimes but they would be treated well if they demonstrated they were "willing to learn the truth." Those who were not willing would be treated as war criminals. They would learn the truth or die in the camp. Execution was frequently mentioned as an outcome for those who did not cooperate. Prisoners had been beaten to death. Prisoners had been forced to stand in the below-zero temperatures until they died. Prisoners were dying every day from lack of food and medical care. POWS at Camp 5 had every reason to believe those threats of execution would be carried out if they did not demonstrate some signs of cooperation. The lecture process lasted seven to ten hours daily, most of that time sitting in the open in the extreme cold. After the actual lectures the POWs had to discuss what they had learned and write an opinion. If they wanted to eat, the opinions had to be positive. Men were placed in the hole for poor attitudes. The sweat box was also a possibility. It was a small cell with three small windows high on one wall and a grill in the door. From four in the morning until eleven at night they had to sit or stand at attention without talking. They had no bed and no blankets. Guards would wake them during the night.

At some point in the spring of 1951 the officers were asked to sign a peace petition. They all refused. The Chinese then said they must debate the issue of the petition and whether or not to sign it. Most finally agreed signing would do no harm as people would understand they were under duress and their names would be made public. Having their names made public increased the chances the Chinese would not execute them. Eight officers still would not sign. These eight were reminded by the Chinese of what had happened to other POWs, reminded of the beatings and the deaths. They were told they would never be released. In the end all the officers signed the petition. The enlisted signed because the officers had signed. Approximately half the camp POW population had died by that time. Even knowing the potential consequences, many signed with phony names or wrote illegibly when they finally signed the petition. Next they were forced to parade through the town of Pyoktong and shout peace slogans. Some prisoners refused to shout the slogans and missed some meals as punishment.

In the summer and fall of 1951 prisoners who did not cooperate during the lectures and the discussions were sometimes hung by their wrists and beaten in full view of their fellow POWs. Most cooperated only as much as was necessary to appease the Chinese. By March of 1952 many POWs felt their names had been released to the United Nations, meaning there was less of a chance they would be killed. One entire company refused to participate any longer in the lectures. From that point the only lectures were for those few prisoners who volunteered for study.

Clothing

POWs arrived in camp wearing whatever they had been captured in minus whatever had been confiscated. In many cases this meant they had no boots. The first clothing issue was not until May 1951 when they were given their standard summer uniform. Until then they had no change of clothing and no baths. In May they were able to bathe in the water of the estuary. The summer clothing issue was every May and the winter issue in September. The summer clothing issue consisted of two pair of light pants, two jackets, one cap, one pair of canvas shoes similar to tennis shoes, two pair of shorts, and two shirts. The winter issue was one pair of cotton padded pants, a padded jacket, and one pair of rubber shoes with cotton padded tops. A POW who arrived at Camp 5 in November 1951 was issued the padded pants and jacket, a cap with flaps, gloves, and the winter shoes. He also received a towel, a bar of soap, toothbrush and tooth powder. If an individual arrived after blankets were issued they did not get one until the next issue of blankets.

Mail

In January of 1952 the first mail was distributed; only a few letters had been handed out prior to then. Prisoners were then allowed to send three letters a month. Mail was handed out two to three times a month but most of the letters were never distributed.

Release

In the first week of August 1953 the POWs were loaded on barges and sent down the Yalu for a few miles, then put in trucks and taken to Sinuiju. From there they traveled in boxcars for a couple of days to Pyongyang and Kaesong. The next leg of the journey home was by truck to a camp a few miles from Panmunjom. They were all searched before leaving Camp 5 and again before being handed over at Panmunjom. The Chinese were especially looking for any lists of POW deaths.

(NARA photo Camp 5).

Part II

Chapter Five

Vietnam Background

The years 1961 to 1973 are commonly used when studying American POWs during the Vietnam War, even though history books generally refer to the years 1964 to 1973 in defining that war. Americans were captured as early as 1954 and as late as 1975.

The organization of Prisoners of War from the Vietnam War, NAM-POWs, refers to 661 military POWs and 141 civilian or foreign POWs. Of these, 472 were held in North Vietnam, 263 in South Vietnam, thirty-one in Laos, thirty-one in Cambodia, and five in China. Some of those POWs held in South Vietnam and some held in Laos were transferred to North Vietnam later in their captivity.

The NAM-POW figures add up to 802, while the Defense Prisoner of War/Missing Personnel Office (DPMO) lists 687 returned, thirty-six escapes, and thirty-seven as died in captivity/remains received. That adds up to 760. A report compiled for the American Ex-Prisoner of War organization lists 114 deaths out of 772 confirmed POWs. Total POW numbers compiled by various organizations differ depending on whether or not civilians and foreign prisoners are included in their figures.

The DPMO lists 687 American Prisoners of War who were returned alive by the Vietnamese from 1961 through 1976. Of this number, seventy-two were returned prior to the release of the bulk of the POWs in Operation Homecoming in 1973. Twelve of these early releases came from North Vietnam. DPMO figures list thirty-six successful escapes, thirty-four of them in South Vietnam and two in Laos.

There were more than those thirty-six escapes, including some from prison camps in Hanoi itself. Some escapes ended in recapture within hours, some individuals were not recaptured for days, and some were simply never seen again. There were individuals who escaped multiple times, in both North and South Vietnam. However, only thirty-six American prisoners of war escaped and then reached U.S. forces. Of those thirty-six successful escapes, twenty-eight of them occurred within the first month of captivity. Only three successful escapes took place after the prisoners had been held more than a year, each of them in the South.

Of the 687 prisoners who returned alive, twenty-four percent were captured in South Vietnam and sixty-eight percent were captured in North Vietnam. The remainder were captured in Laos, Cambodia, and China. The majority of the seventy-two early releases, fifty-seven of them, were released in the years 1967 through 1970. Of the 687 returned POWs, 117 (seventeen percent) were enlisted and fifty-six were civilian. The remaining 514 (seventy-five percent) were officers, the large majority of which were pilots.

There were only three Americans actually rescued from captivity during the entire war. One died shortly after rescue from wounds inflicted by his guards before they ran from the rescue forces. The second was an unplanned rescue which took place while the prisoner was being escorted from his point of capture to a prison camp. The third (also unplanned) involved a helicopter assault in an area which turned out to hold prisoners. An American POW broke loose and ran to the helicopters. There were many attempts to rescue American POWs, the most well known being the attack on the camp at Son Tay in North Vietnam. After the war there were cases where prisoners reported they had been within sight and sound of American rescue forces but were prevented by their guards from taking any action. There were about 500 South Vietnamese soldiers freed in these rescue attempts.

In August of 1965 the International Committee of the Red Cross asked all combatants in Southeast Asia to observe the Geneva Conventions concerning treatment of POWs. The United States and South Vietnam agreed to do so. North Vietnam and the Viet Cong did not. With only one exception, Red Cross inspections were not allowed in any POW camps in South East Asia controlled by the North Vietnamese or their allies. North Vietnam presented the point of view that since no war had been declared, the captives they held were war criminals and not protected under the Geneva Convention. The North Vietnamese stated again and again, that, although the Geneva Convention did not apply, they were treating the war criminals in a humane and lenient manner. The definition of humane and lenient was given to one American POW who had been severely beaten and then forced to remain on his knees for hours, a standard torture technique. His interrogator allowed the POW a five-minute break from this position each hour because of the prisoner's leg infection. The interrogator told the POW this was in accordance with the humane and lenient treatment policy of the Vietnamese people.

During the war there was frequent mention in the media that Americans held by North Vietnam were being "brainwashed," a fear left over from Korea. (There was almost no mention in the media about those Americans held in South Vietnam or Laos.) Even among the POWs in Hanoi, there was concern some fellow prisoners were too easily writing statements or making broadcasts. Eventually the senior ranking officers recognized the impossibility of anyone withstanding the torture techniques of the North Vietnamese. Orders were given that individuals were to endure what they could and then try to minimize any statement they signed or broadcast they made. On the return of the POWs in 1973 there were no FBI investigations. The Joint Chiefs of Staff decided there would be no courts martial. What was endured by the POWs from Korea would not be inflicted on the POWs from Vietnam.

Chapter Six

South Vietnam—Conditions

There were some major differences for prisoners held in the South versus those held in the North. Prisoners in the South were typically younger enlisted men. They were kept in smaller groups and had little contact with other Americans. Some POWs in the South went for months, even years, without contact with another American. When they did, it was with small groups only.

POWs in the South died at a greater rate than prisoners held in the North. Twenty to twenty-five percent (depending on the source) of POWs held in the South died versus five percent of those held in the North. The farther south a POW was held captive the higher the risks to his health. Fifty percent of the POWs held in the Mekong Delta area did not survive their captivity.

Conditions in these camps may be better understood with the following example: It was not unusual for guards to keep a few chickens or pigs as part of their food supply. In one camp a pig took to eating the fecal mess caused by ever-present diarrhea. At times the pig would spot a prisoner preparing to squat for a bowel movement and actually lick the prisoner's anus as he defecated. The POWs became accustomed to this practice.

POW camps in the South were usually little more than crude huts or cages. Food and medical supplies were much more limited than what was available in the North. POWs held in the more northern provinces of South Vietnam were more likely to be transferred into North Vietnam at some point, improving their chances for survival. One hundred and two POWs released in Hanoi during Operation Homecoming in 1973 had been captured and held in the South. When they arrived in Northern camps they saw their lives as having been improved. They considered the food to be better in quantity and quality and the living conditions better than what they had experienced in the South. On the other hand, POWs held in the South were more likely to be released. Of the seventy-two early releases during the war, sixty were prisoners held in Southern POW camps.

It was in South Vietnam that the longest held American POW of the war was captured. Army Captain Floyd (Jim) Thompson was captured 26 March 1964. He was moved to North Vietnam in the summer of 1968 and released from Hanoi in Operation Homecoming on 16 March 1973.

Housing

POW camps holding Americans prisoner in the South did not have housing; they had shelter. This shelter was commonly a few simple thatch huts for the guards and bamboo cages for the Americans. The cages were frequently only large enough to allow the prisoner to sit up or lie flat and the bed was the bamboo or dirt floor of the cage. At one time or another in their captivity, many prisoners held in the South were kept isolated in a single bamboo cage. If not alone, they were typically kept out of sight and sound of other Americans also held in that camp.

Replica of a POW cage used in the South as seen in the National POW Museum in Andersonville, Georgia.

Some prisoners were held in groups of twelve or fifteen. One camp for a group this size consisted of bamboo huts surrounded by a bamboo fence. Inside the enclosure were guard huts, a prisoner hut, and a latrine pit. The prisoners slept on a bamboo platform about three feet off the ground. Designed for five or six, the platform had to accommodate many more held there at different times. (Eleven of the approximately thirty POWs eventually held there died.) This camp included an open-air classroom used for political lectures. In another camp the prisoners slept in hammocks in cages set below ground level.

Southern camps were typically located in dismal swamps or triple canopy forests. Actual sunlight was so rare prisoners would argue about who could sit in whatever rays managed to penetrate to the forest floor. The location alone could be detrimental to the health of the POWs. These camps were open to the elements. Malaria was common in Southern POW camps, as were fungal infections, leeches, snakes, scorpions, centipedes, and ants. One POW described a particular camp in the South as "hideous, muddy, leech and insect-filled". In the monsoon season the camps would be a sea of mud. With the common problem of dysentery, and people frequently not making it to the latrine pit before a bowel movement, this mud became a sea of filth.

Treatment

In the very early years of the war, a prisoner held in the South was likely to be treated fairly well and released within a few months. As the war progressed this practice changed. POWs were frequently neglected or mistreated.

At some point the POWs might be given a mat, blanket, and mosquito net. This might occur as soon as they arrived at a camp, or they might be forced to go without for a few days or weeks so they would appreciate the "humane and lenient" treatment of their captors. In one camp no mosquito nets or blankets were made available for the first two years of captivity. In some cases the blankets provided were made from used rice sacks. A crude form of soap was sometimes made available. Small towels would be issued, as would what Westerners called "pajamas", the standard clothing of the region. As these items were used up or worn out they might, or might not, be replaced. Shoes or boots were commonly taken from the POWs. On difficult journeys between camps, they might be allowed to use the standard VC sandal; more often they marched in bare feet.

It was not unusual for the prisoners to be tied or shackled while in their cages, especially if being punished. Severe punishment would mean being shackled in the hut or cage twenty-four hours a day for days, made to lie in their own urine and excrement. In these instances their mosquito nets might also be taken away. This treatment, as well as beatings, reduced food rations, and neglecting injuries and illnesses was the torture of the Southern POW camps.

The type of physical torture applied on a regular basis in the North was not found in Southern camps. A prisoner might be beaten for an escape attempt or some other behavior, but more extreme torture was not common in the South. It was not necessary. The severe conditions of the camps-disease, malnutrition, isolation, boredom, even artillery and bombing by US forces, all were used as tools by the VC to get what they wanted from the prisoners. What they wanted were written appeals for the prisoner's release, letters condemning the war, or anti-war statements. The VC pushed constantly for letters or recordings they could use for propaganda purposes. Seldom were they asked for useful military information. POWs were continually lectured to about the "correct" actions of the National Liberation Front and the "in-correct" actions of the US. (The National Liberation Front was the political arm of the resistance movement in the South, the Viet Cong the military arm.) If the POWs could not be used for some sort of propaganda purpose they had little value to their captors.

In their attempts to gain written statements from the prisoners, the guards would require them to publicly criticize other prisoners. Subtle pressures were applied to pit prisoner against prisoner by focusing on race relations in the US and among the prisoners, conduct of lower ranks towards senior NCOs and officers, guard promises of medical care for wounds or illnesses, even offers of better food for better behavior.

It was not often POWs in the South were required to work. Depending on the size of the camp and the availability of food, they might be made to chop wood for cooking fires, help construct shelters, plant gardens, forage for food, or fish in nearby streams or canals.

POWs were moved from camp to camp during the period of their captivity. A prisoner might be held in six or seven different camps in as many months. At times they would return to an old camp. A camp might have to be abandoned due to US operations in the vicinity. The prisoner, or prisoners, would be marched to a new location, sometimes helping to build their new camp.

Medical Care

POWs held in the South experienced a range of health problems including anemia, beriberi, bleeding gums, dysentery, eczema, edema, gingivitis, lost teeth, malaria, osteomalacia, scurvy, and a skin fungus. This fungus could be so severe as to cover almost the entire body. The resulting scratching led to infections. Osteomalacia (a softening of the bones caused by long-term deficiency of calcium), digestive disorders, and poorly functioning kidneys were all a direct result of the poor diet and lack of sun-light common to Southern camps. Weight loss could be as much as half the prisoner's body weight at capture.

If the POWs were held close to a major Viet Cong (VC) base camp, they might receive treatment for wounds or illnesses there. Even in those circumstances, wounds were likely to become infected with maggots before any treatment was given. The one medical doctor captured in the South, a US army captain, was not allowed "...to practice medicine unless a man was 30 minutes away from dying..."

Injuries and illnesses were often used as bargaining tools by the VC. A prisoner would be told treatment would be made available if they demonstrated a cooperative attitude. Prisoners who were very ill or had serious wounds and were considered "resisters" were likely to be killed. It was only in the South that prisoners were executed and those executions publicly acknowledged by the VC. Many other POW deaths were caused by simple neglect on the part of their captors. Wounds and illnesses which did not have to be life threatening were made so by the failure of the VC to take preventive action. It could be argued that this failure was not always purposeful, but simply a fact of life for the VC themselves. POWs did receive rudimentary care when it fit the purposes of their captors. Injections of penicillin or vitamins were common treatments for many medical problems. Sulfa and quinine were at times made available to the POWs. Other times nothing would be provided. Either result seemed to depend as much on the attitude of the guards at the camp as the availability of the drugs.

Food

The standard menu in the South was rice, two or three cups a day. Since the POW camps were in remote swamps or jungle forests, and since camps had to be moved frequently, rice could not be grown locally. The rice fed to the POWs had been transported long distances and stored for long periods of time. This meant the rice received by POWs in the South was rotten and full of bugs and rat feces. When supply lines were disrupted the rice ration had to be supplemented with whatever was available. At various times POWs ate elephant, ape, snake, dog, and rat. The guards would add protein to their own meals with chickens, eggs, and pork, when available. Occasionally they would allow some of these items to be included in the POW meals, but not on a regular basis. In one camp the POWs killed the cat kept as a pet by the guards. Before they could eat it they were caught and punished.

The meals would sometimes have greens added to them. These greens would be grown in a small garden in the camp or found on foraging trips around the camp area. POWs would often take part in this foraging. Manioc (a potato-like tuber) was searched for and brought back to camp by the armful. Wood to use in cooking fires was also gathered. With the POWs already malnourished, these foraging trips often used more calories than they gained from the food gathered. With no shoes, their feet were easily injured and infections often followed.

In camps with more than a few American POWs, the prisoners cooked their own food. In cases where only a few prisoners were in the camp, the guards would prepare all the meals. POWs could see meat and greens added to the guards' meals which did not appear in their own.

When POWs were going to be released, they would be fed better in the days or weeks before hand. In camps where there were a number of American POWs, a ceremony would be held before the release. At this time all kinds of meats and sweets, even cans of condensed milk, would be part of the menu. At Christmas the guards might give the prisoners candy. In one case, the prisoners were given one can of condensed milk to share among the entire group of about twelve. This was likely not an example of a cruel joke, but an indication of the lack of food available to even the guards. Starvation was a major factor in deaths of POWs held in the South, either directly or by causing diseases incurred from a weakened immune system.

Mail

Prisoners held in the South might have been able to get a message or letter out of their camp when a fellow POW was released. Letters might be written but seldom if ever actually sent. A few letters from home were given to POWs early in the war.

Red Cross

There were no inspections allowed by the International Committee of the Red Cross. In the spring of 1965 the four American POWs held in one camp were given one Red Cross parcel each. This appears to be the only case of Red Cross parcels being distributed to POWs held in the South.

Death Marches

As the Bataan Death March in the Philippines, the deadly marches through the cold and snow in Germany, and the Tiger Death March in Korea, so too did Vietnam have its own death marches. The difference was the marches were by individuals or very small groups. Prisoners were continually marched from one camp to another throughout the war. In many cases they had no shoes or only simple sandals. They were physically exhausted and medically unfit for such strenuous activity. Prisoners died on the trail and prisoners were executed on the trail. In the case of POWs being marched into North Vietnam there were deaths caused by US attacks on the Ho Chi Minh Trail complex. For every case of POWs being carried on makeshift stretchers by their captors to aid stations there are three or four examples of death or execution at the hands of those same captors. As in the death marches of previous wars, there were POWs who begged to be shot rather than have to continue the pain of forcing their exhausted and disease-ridden bodies farther down the trail. As in previous wars, it will never be known how many Americans died alone on Southeast Asian jungle paths.

Chapter Seven

South Vietnam — The Camps

Delta/U Minh Area

The southernmost camps were about 150 miles southwest of Saigon in the U Minh forest region. These were located in thick swamps. The conditions of these camps can be seen in the names given to them by the POWs. They called them Mangrove Motel, No-K Corral, Salt Mines, Neverglades, and Mosquito Junction. In most of these camps the POWs were held in individual cages. At No-K Corral they were housed in a single cage which was too small for anyone to stand up. Neverglades was an improvement in that they were kept in open huts. When the POWs (those captured 1963-65) first arrived at Neverglades it was the first time in sixteen months they were in a camp on solid ground. Beri beri, dysentery, malaria, malnutrition, and skin fungus were common. Since the prisoners were not held all at the same time or all at the same camp, some individuals were held in their bamboo cage for months without seeing another American. One spent a year and a half in a four foot high cage in a leg iron almost twenty-four hours a day.

Prisoners held here included: Gerasimo Arroyo-Baez, John Graf, James Jackson, Edward Johnson, Joseph Parks, Daniel Pitzer, King Rayford, James Rowe, Leonard Tadios, Humberto Versace, OJ Walker, and Robert White. White was released from the area in 1973, the last American released in Operation Homecoming. King Rayford was released in Hanoi in 1973.

Escaped: Rowe
Executed: Versace
Died: Arroyo-Baez, Parks, Tadios, Walker
Killed in escape attempt: Graf
Released Early: Jackson, Johnson, Pitz

Parrot's Beak/Schrump Group

Beginning in early 1968 American POWs were held in a series of camps they named Alpha through Echo along the Cambodian border in the Parrot's Beak region west of Tay Ninh. Camps Hotel through Lima were inside Cambodia. They were held for a few weeks or a few months at a camp and then moved on. At Bravo they were kept together in huts and chained together at night. They moved after an air strike hit the camp. Camp Charlie in August 1968 was at first a five foot deep pit dug in the ground and covered with logs. Then they were kept in nine by eight foot cages, not big enough to stand upright. In September, at Camp Delta, they spent six months with no shelters and slept chained in hammocks. They were kept thirty feet apart, with the jungle foliage so thick they often could not see one another. Exercise was allowed and they could bathe in the stream. For entertainment they had nightly English radio broadcasts from Hanoi. After an escape in March of 1969 the group was moved to Camp Echo. Echo was also known as Monkey Cages. There they spent a year in cages set below ground. Two prisoners spent a month locked in those cages for punishment. The soil at Monkey Cages was poor and food was always insufficient. Rats were used to supplement the diet. Monsoon rains flooded the underground cages. Malaria was a problem as were anemia, beri beri, and dysentery.

In the spring of 1970 more prisoners were added to the group. In March the four civilians (Brookens, Kjome, Rollins, and Utecht) were sent to the group held in the Tay Ninh area. In the summer they were in Cambodia in cages again, this time above ground. The group spent the next two years moving back and forth among these camps, sometimes enduring helicopter gunship attacks and B-52 bomb drops. In late January 1973 both of these groups were joined together near Kratie, Cambodia. In February they were trucked back into South Vietnam for release at Loc Ninh on 12 Feb 1973.

Prisoners held here included: Norm Brookens, John Dunn, Kenneth Gregory, Charles Hyland, Thomas Jones, Tanos Kalil, Mike Kjome, Jim Rollins, James Ray, Raymond Schrump, Dick Utecht, and Thomas Vanputten. In early 1970 the following joined the group-Frederic Crowson, Walter Ferguson, Gary Guggenberger, James Hestand, Bobby Johnson, Daniel Maslowski, Felix Neco-Quinones, Ferdinand Rodriquez,

John Sexton, Richard Springman, Michael Varnado, Richard Waldhaus, Robert Young.

Escaped: Vanputten
Died: Ferguson, Kalil, Ray, Varnado, Young
Released Early: Gregory, Jones, Hyland, Sexton

Tay Ninh

Another group of camps was located northwest of Saigon in the area near Tay Ninh along the Cambodian border. There were ten camps with names such as Sing Sing, Bivouac, Auschwitz, Baffle, Little Stream, Big Stream, and Carefree. Carefree was also called Paradise, but the third name given to it was less tongue-in-cheek - Dachau. Prisoners on their way to this area were held in temporary camps dubbed San Jose and SOB. POWs were held in this area beginning in January 1964. Until the summer of 1965 there were only four: Camacho, McClure, Roraback, and Smith. Each was given a set of the standard "pajamas", a mosquito net, a tin cup, aluminum plate, and a spoon. All this was rolled in their hammock when moving through the jungle. For a few weeks the four had only hammocks in the jungle for shelter while they were lectured daily about the war. In early 1964 at Auschwitz they were held separately in four large cages in a VC base camp area. They called the cages "slammers", referring to jail cells. The guard hut was in the center with the POW cages around that. Four wells had been dug in the area so bucket showers were available regularly. The prisoners were allowed to move about the area during the day but locked up in the cages again at night. They were sometimes led into the thick jungle surrounding the camp to cut and chop firewood. Food was made available in sufficient quantity but the quality led to malnutrition. They dealt with bad water, bugs, snakes, hot days, and cold nights. Very little direct sunlight reached the jungle floor. They were under constant pressure to write anti-war statements.

In September 1964 they were at Little Stream, chained at night to a common post in the same hut with the guards. After three weeks they moved to Big Stream. By the end of 1964 the area was flooded and they moved back to Auschwitz where they found bomb craters from an attack during their absence. This time they were kept in two cages and tied by one ankle each night to a post. Fox holes were dug by the POWs to use as shelters from the many fighter-bomber attacks in the area. Next came Carefree where at least some of the POWs were given letters from home. Iron Mines may have been another name for this camp, a reference to the difficulty in digging the air raid shelters.

In early 1965 some Red Cross parcels were handed out to the group. Early in the summer Cook, Crafts, and Schuman were brought into the camp. In July 1965 Camacho escaped, prompting all those still in camp to be chained day and night in their cages. Shortly after the escape the camp was moved again, this time to Camp Baffle. At Baffle a large cage was built with a bamboo and thorn fence around it. Then a second cage was built for the two POWs who were officers. It was here that Roraback was executed. In November 1965 McClure and Smith were released.

The POWs in this area were not always held in the same camp at the same time. From fall 1966 to late 1967 some of them were kept in cages dug in the ground which were flooded by the monsoon rains. This camp was in an area with poor soil which resulted in a poor diet. These conditions led to anemia, beri beri, dysentery, and malaria. Refusing indoctrination attempts meant chains and no food. Some spent months unaware new prisoners had been brought into the camp. At times they were chained twenty-four hours a day and other times they were free to move around. In some locations they were kept in large cages and other times they had only hammocks. Douglas Ramsey and Sammie Womack joined the group in the middle of 1966. Crafts and Womack were released in February 1967. William Hardy came into camp that September. In late 1967 they were moved closer to the Cambodian border. Cook died during this move. In early 1969 John Fritz, James Newingham, and Tanos Kalil were made part of the group. By fall 1969 they had been moved across the border into Cambodia. A year later the group was at a camp farther inside Cambodia and away from the constant fighting along the border area. In April 1970 four POWs from the Schrump group were brought into camp (Brookens, Kjome, Rollins, and Utecht). Keith Albert arrived in February 1971. Two months later the group was moved near Kratie. By this time, those men captured in 1964 had been held in as many as twenty different camps. At the end of January 1973 they were joined by the Schrump group and all were trucked back into South Vietnam for release at Loc Ninh on 12 Feb 1973.

Prisoners held here included: Keith Albert, Harold Bennett, Norm Brookens, Issac Camacho, Donald Cook, Charles Crafts, John Fritz,

William Hardy, Tanos Kalil, Michael Kjome, Claude McClure, James
Newingham, Douglas Ramsey, James Rollins, Kenneth Roraback,
John Schuman, George Smith, Richard Utecht, and Sammie Womack.
Escaped: Camacho
Executed: Roraback
Died: Bennett, Cook, Kalil, and Schuman
Released Early: Crafts, McClure, Smith, Womack

In early November 1969 Luis Chirichigno, James Nowicki,
Michael Peterson, and Vernon Shepard were captured and held near
the Cambodian border directly west of Nha Trang. They were kept in
bunkers dug about three feet deep with bamboo poles for sides and
thatch roofs. The bunkers, about 8' by 15' in size, were surrounded by
an eight foot high pole fence and punji stakes. Each bunker had a door
with a lock of some kind and ankle stocks. Several South Vietnamese
Army POWs were held in bunkers in the same complex. This small
camp was probably typical of the many camps throughout South Vietnam which held a few POWs on a temporary basis until they were sent
on to one of the more permanent camps. Peterson and Shepard were
released on 10 December and Chirichigno and Nowicki sent to Hanoi,
possibly with the Tri-Border group.

Camps 101/102 Tri-Border Area

Farther north from Tay Ninh is the tri-border area where Laos, Cambodia, and Vietnam meet. From about July of 1967 until late 1969 about twenty POWs were held first at Camp 101 and then nearby Camp 102. The names 101 and 102 may have come from numbers on writing paper the guards used. The camps were only a few miles apart in a VC/NVA base camp area west of Kontum near the Cambodian border. Camp 101 may have been just inside Vietnam. The POW huts were really cages made of bamboo. Camp 101 was surrounded by a bamboo fence. Both camps were small in area with just a few cages for the prisoners and huts for the guards. The POW cages were locked shut at night. The guard huts were positioned so they could observe the prisoners at all times. One guard was always situated in a "guard shack" at the only exit through the fence around the camp. Bowing to the guards was mandatory.

The two meals a day were poor and the POWs were locked in their cages except for brief periods to exercise and use the latrine. In the first few months at 101 no exercise was allowed at all. Prisoners would rise about 0600 to use the latrine and eat breakfast and then have to sit in their cages all day. At night their legs were placed in crude ankle stocks. Talking was usually forbidden so they would "sing" information to each other, as the guards usually ignored singing. When they displayed poor attitudes during political lectures they were placed in solitary cages. Like other POWs in the south, they received no medical care for their anemia, beri beri, dehydration, dengue fever, dysentery, malaria, malnutrition, pneumonia, and scurvy. After an escape attempt in October 1967 the six POWs there at the time were kept in stocks twenty-four hours a day except for two latrine breaks.

Interrogation sessions were held for the first month or so. Indoctrination sessions were held for three hours at a time every two months. During those sessions they were lectured on the history of Vietnam.

In February 1968 they were moved from 101 to nearby 102, on a mountain top inside Cambodia. The cages at Camp 102 were surrounded by two bamboo and barbed wire fences with punji stakes -

sharpened bamboo - placed about knee high in rows in the ground in between the fences. Ankle stocks were used here as at Camp 101, but by the summer of 1968 they were allowed out of the stocks again during the day. Bathing was allowed in a stream about once a week. More POWs were brought into the camp during 1968. They were not allowed to mix with each other but could talk carefully from cage to cage. On 8 November 1969 the prisoners held at Camp 102 were sent north in two separate groups, arriving at Farnsworth near Hanoi around Christmas.

Prisoners held here included: Michael Benge, Henry Blood, Lenard Daugherty, Joe DeLong, Peter Drabic, Martin Frank, Robert Grzyb, Nathan Henry, Thomas Horio, Juan Jacquez, Gail Kerns, Stephen Leopold, Don MacPhail, Cordine McMurray, Stanley Newell, Betty Olsen, Richard Perricone, William Smith, David Sooter, James Van Bendegom.

Died: Blood, Grzyb, Olsen, Smith, Van Bendegom

Van Bendegom actually died in a field hospital at a VC base camp where he and Frank, Henry, McMurray, Newell, and Perricone were held before being sent to Camp 101. William Smith died on the trail when the group was sent north.

Killed in escape attempt: DeLong

Benge, Blood, and Olsen were held west of Nha Trang in the spring and summer of 1968 until their move to Camp 102. Blood and Olsen died during the move, prior to reaching 102.

Robert Grzyb is referred to by Nathan Henry as Robert Zebulan and Robert Zeb in the Vinson book, *To Hell and Beyond*. Martin Frank referred to him as Robert Zebb in his debrief found in the Library of Congress POW/MIA database. That database has a Robert Zebb listed with no additional information available. There was no Robert Zebb. Robert Grzyb was a former Army draftee/enlistee living illegally as a civilian in Pleiku when captured.

Tam Ky/Kushner Group

POWs were held in a series of at least four camps in this area. The camps were between Tam Ky (just south of Da Nang) and the Cambodia border. Each of the camps was similar in its layout - thick jungle, a stream nearby, bamboo huts on a hilltop enclosed by a bamboo fence. One of the camps had an area of about thirty by ninety feet surrounded by a bamboo fence. Within that area was a single hut for the POWs that had a six foot wide bamboo sleeping platform with a three foot walking space around it. In the hut was a small fire pit and a latrine pit. The sleeping platform allowed only enough space for each man to lie completely straight. They slept on the bamboo platform with no mats. No mosquito nets were issued and the prisoners had only the clothing they were captured in. (When two new POWs arrived in the late spring of 1968, a second hut was added for the prisoners. POWs then included Anton, Cannon, Daly, Davis, Garwood, Grissett, Hammond, Harker, Kushner, McMillan, Pfister, Sherman, Strictland, Watkins, Weatherman, Williams, and Zawtocki.) A classroom with benches was constructed for indoctrination sessions, some of which lasted six hours a day.

Twice a week some of the group would go out into the jungle to gather firewood and food. The meals were usually rice and manioc. Cooking was done by the POWs themselves. The only time they had sufficient food was when a celebration was held for those being released. This only happened twice. Very small amounts of meat were included in meals only two or three times a year. The lack of food, and vitamins in the food, led to a loss of strength that made even walking to the stream to bathe difficult. Night blindness was also a problem.

Each afternoon there was a head count of the prisoners and guards checked on them every three hours during the night. Regular political lectures were conducted, during which time they were supposed to point out faults of themselves or their fellow prisoners. They also had to listen to the Voice of Vietnam on a camp radio. The VC officials who conducted the lectures were constantly trying to turn the African-American and Mexican-American prisoners against the war. The POWs were kept at Bravo all of 1968 and the first five months of

1969. Six of them died in the last months of 1968. Food quantities grew less and monsoon rains turned the area to a mixture of mud and feces. Dysentery, malaria, and a skin fungus caused serious problems for all POWs held here. The fungus drove the prisoners to scratching, which caused bleeding and the release of pus, bringing flies, followed by maggots.

In August of 1968 there were twenty-one prisoners in the camp. With the deaths in late 1968 and the arrival of new POWs, the camp held seventeen by March 1969. The last eight months of 1969 they were kept at Camp Charlie where four West German nurses captured near Da Nang joined them. (A fifth nurse had died a few weeks before and two died after just a few months at this camp. The surviving two were moved to a different camp in September 1969.) At this location they were again in one hut in a fenced-in area, the fence being of bamboo. The next move was to Camp Delta at the end of December. Two more died from December to March. At Delta they experienced artillery strikes, B-52 strikes, and a helicopter assault almost on top of the camp. Food for the prisoners at this camp often came from the grain supply for the pigs. The POW shelter was larger than before and indoctrination classes were still held. In early February 1971 the twelve surviving prisoners of the group were sent north, arriving at the Plantation in Hanoi after a two month journey. The first part of the march north was on foot on the Ho Chi Minh trail where they slept in pre-built bunkers along the way. Once in Vietnam they traveled by truck to Vinh and then by train to Hanoi. Of the approximately thirty prisoners held here over the years, eleven died, five were released early, and one was killed in an escape attempt.

Prisoners held here included: Jose Agostos- Santos, Jose Anzaldua, Frank Anton, Georg Bartsch, Fred Burns, Francis Cannon, James Daly, Thomas Davis, Bernhard Diehl, William Eisenbraun, Fred Elbert, Robert Garwood, Russell Grissett, Dennis Hammond, David Harker, Hindrika Kortman, Floyd Kushner, Robert Lewis, Julius Long, Isiah McMillan, Gustav Mehrer, Luis Ortiz-Rivera, James Pfister, William Port, Monica Schwinn, Robert Sherman, James Strickland, Coy Tinsley, Willie Watkins, Earl Weatherman, Richard Williams, and Joseph Zawtocki. Bartsch, Diehl, Kortman, and Schwinn were West German nurses working as volunteers.

Executed: Weatherman (evidently killed after escape attempt)

Died: Bartsch, Burns, Cannon, Eisenbraun, Grissett, Hammond, Kortman, Port, Sherman, Williams, and Zawtocki.

Released early: Agostos-Santos, Ortiz-Rivera, Strickland, Tinsley, and Watkins.

Defected to the enemy: Robert Garwood

Laos/DMZ Area

Captain Floyd (Jim) Thompson was held in a series of about twelve camps he labeled according to the military phonetic alphabet-Alpha, Bravo, and so on. These camps were in the Khe Sanh area of far northwestern South Vietnam and across the border into Laos. From his capture in March 1964 until his arrival at Bao Cao in North Vietnam during the fall of 1967 he saw no other Americans. He was constantly lectured on the history of Vietnam and pressured to make recorded statements. His housing was a bamboo cage in the jungle which brought frequent attacks of malaria. At Foxtrot the guards did what they could to make life miserable by removing his blanket and placing him in a poorly constructed hut. At Golf, in August 1967, he was kept in a large village somewhere near Bao Cao. His bed was a narrow board on blocks. He was given no mosquito net and kept in leg irons. At one point here he was given the ropes treatment common at the Hanoi Hilton. Another time he was hung by his thumbs.

He arrived in the Bao Cao area in the fall of 1967 and kept chained in a small cage. When he would not bow as demanded by the guards he was beaten. In the spring of 1968 he was moved into the camp with the other Americans.

After the 1968 Tet Offensive, prisoners captured in and around Da Nang and Hue were held for a short period of time in the area until they were moved into North Vietnam. In their initial move away from the coast the prisoners were roped together with their hands tied behind their backs. Most of their clothing and their shoes were taken away. They were held at Camp Runamuck 1 for about four weeks. The name was used by the civilian POWs but apparently not the military prisoners. The camp was only a few hours walk from Hue. The prisoners were kept in a twenty to thirty-foot long bunker dug into the mountain side and covered with thatch and foliage. They had to sleep in shifts as there was not enough room for all to stretch out. The food was described by Lewis Meyer as "rice, rocks, bugs, and rat dung with a definite shortage on the rice." At the end of February the group set out on foot to North Vietnam. Along the way two POWs escaped. After a four to five day walk, sleeping on the ground along the way, the group spent a week near the Laotian border at Camp Runamuck 2.

They were housed in a large bamboo structure with a thatch roof. When they complained about the food to the camp commander his wife took over the cooking for them. They were allowed to build a fireplace in their hut to keep warm at night. The camp was on the highest mountain in the area. The group left for the North on the 11th or 12th of March, most of them, if not all, headed next to Bao Cao. Both of the Runamuck locations were staging areas used by the NVA to move their troops into South Vietnam, not specific POW camps.

Prisoners held here included: Cloden Adkins, John Anderson, Candido Badua, Art Balagot, Marc Cayer (Canadian), Gary Daves, John Deering, James DiBernardo, Edward Dierling, Harry Ettmueller, Solomon Godwin, Theodore Gostas, Donat Gouin, Robert Hayhurst, Alexander Henderson, Sandra Johnson, Philip Manhard, Lewis Meyer, Marjorie Nelson, Michael O'Connor, Robert Olsen, Russell Page, Thomas Ragsdale, Donald Rander, Thomas Rushton, Everett Siddons, Richard Spaulding, Lawrence Stark, Eugene Weaver, and Charles Willis.

Escaped: Dierling and Hayhurst

Died: Godwin and Ragsdale (Ragsdale was killed in a bombing raid while the group was held for a few days at a major supply depot that came under attack)

Released early: Johnson and Nelson

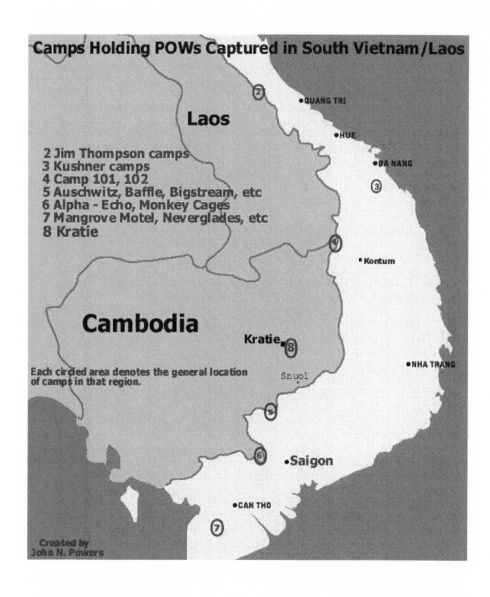

Camps Holding POWs Captured in South Vietnam/Laos

Laos

QUANG TRI
HUE
DA NANG

2 Jim Thompson camps
3 Kushner camps
4 Camp 101, 102
5 Auschwitz, Baffle, Bigstream, etc
6 Alpha - Echo, Monkey Cages
7 Mangrove Motel, Neverglades, etc
8 Kratie

Kontum

Cambodia

Kratie

Each circled area denotes the general location
of camps in that region.

Snuol

NHA TRANG

Saigon

CAN THO

Created by
John N. Powers

Chapter Eight

North Vietnam — Conditions

Americans held prisoner in North Vietnam experienced boredom, discomfort, hunger, isolation, and torture over the period of their captivity. Each of these conditions was deliberately imposed on the POWs by their Vietnamese captors. Until late 1970 the Vietnamese kept the POWs as isolated as possible. They accomplished this isolation by maintaining a number of camps scattered throughout northern Vietnam. Some of them held only ten or fifteen prisoners. There were compounds within camps, all kept separated from each other. Communication of any kind was generally forbidden and severe punishment administered to those who ignored that rule. The Vietnamese wanted every individual prisoner to feel abandoned and alone. Constant pressure was applied on individuals to write or record statements against the war which could be shown to other POWs or printed in Communist or Western publications. If a POW felt alone it was easier for his interrogators to convince that prisoner to give in to their demands for propaganda material. Many prisoners went months, and some went years, without face-to-face communication with another American. During the years 1965 through 1970 the use of torture was common. That meant deliberately inflicting severe physical pain on the POWs and frequently included confinement in a bare, completely darkened cell with nothing but the floor for a bed.

After 1970 some changes took place. The Vietnamese seemed to ease up on (but not completely abandon) their practice of torture and improved the food and living conditions somewhat. Three events are seen as catalysts for these changes. In September 1969 Ho Chi Minh died and three POWs released by the North Vietnamese held a press conference. For the first time, the released POWs talked publicly about their treatment as prisoners, especially the torture. The press conference and Ho's death occurred within a few days of each other. The North Vietnamese felt world opinion turning against them and apparently used Ho's death in an attempt to change their status from aggressor to more of a victim.

The third event took place late in 1970. In November of that year a force of about 60 Americans penetrated to within twenty-five miles of Hanoi, landed on North Vietnamese soil, and assaulted the prisoner of war camp at Son Tay. They were prepared to rescue and return to US control about seventy American POWs. They found none. Within days of that raid the Vietnamese were moving most of their prisoners into camps within Hanoi. This required housing the POWs together in large groups, something they had tried to avoid prior to that time. Some POWs went from having no cell mate or one cell mate to having twenty or thirty. For the first time POWs could talk freely with fellow prisoners they had been communicating with only by taps on a wall.

By the last half of 1972 the Vietnamese knew the war was almost over. Food and medical care improved and more physical activity was allowed. The prisoners were being fattened up to show the world how well they had been treated under the humane and lenient policies of the North Vietnamese.

Housing

Three types of cells were common. A two man cell contained two beds and measured about seven feet by seven feet. The beds were wooden pallets or cement platforms raised about eighteen inches off the floor. In some cells were wooden or iron ankle stocks. Normally, the only other piece of furniture was a latrine bucket. There was a two foot wide aisle between the bunks. A small wattage light bulb might remain on twenty-four hours a day. The cells typically had high walls with small windows or vent holes at the top. This meant very little air movement.

The second type of cell was larger, up to twenty by forty-five feet. It would hold eight, twenty, or even forty prisoners. A raised concrete sleeping platform, again about eighteen inches high, was in the center of the cell with about a two and a half foot space around it. If there was room, all the prisoners slept on the platform. If not, some slept in the walk space. These cells were only used in Unity the last two years of the war.

The third type of cell was the single cell used for punishment or for isolating the senior officers and hard-line resisters. Frequently these had no light bulb and were boarded up to limit light from outside as well as restrict air movement.

Photo of a two-man cell in the Hanoi Hilton Museum in Hanoi. The windows would have been boarded over from 1965 until 1970, when treatment improved. (Courtesy of Renate Ecker.)

These were the standard cells, with frequent variations of each type. Common to almost any cell were the very large rats, mice, cockroaches, mosquitoes, lack of air movement, heat of 120 degrees or more in the summer, and cold as low as forty or fifty degrees in the winter.

For the most part, only the cells in the Hanoi Hilton were the standard western image of prison cells. The Hilton included a real prison with cells and heavy iron doors. The number of prisoners soon outgrew the number of cells available. New cells were built in other parts of the Hilton and then other buildings around Hanoi. Although the North Vietnamese built these new cells to keep the prisoners isolated there were usually one or two cracks in the doors or boarded-over windows that allowed some form of communication. In some cases the POWs actually used iron rods to bore small holes through cell walls to whisper back and forth.

Treatment

If there was a typical day for an American prisoner of war in North Vietnam it might have started with a gong at 5 or 5:30 am. At 6 Hanoi Hannah and the program the Voice of Vietnam were broadcast over the camp speakers. Sometime in the morning a prisoner would be allowed to take out his latrine bucket to empty and clean it. This was done on a schedule meant to keep POWs from seeing each other. The first meal was issued about 10 am, the second about 4:30 pm. Until 1971 there was no third meal. A gong sounded about 9 pm as a signal to go to bed. A bath might be allowed, unless the prisoner was being punished, there was a water shortage, it was too cold, or some other reason the guards might have. A bath could mean washing with a rag and a bucket or standing under water flowing from a pipe in the wall. Bathing only once every couple of weeks was common. The Voice of Vietnam was broadcast again in the evening.

There was a standard issue of clothing and supplies given to each POW, usually shortly after their arrival in Hanoi. They were given two sets of long sleeve shirts and pants and two sets of short sleeved shirts and shorts. These were the striped prison clothes referred to as pajamas. Each prisoner was given one pair of rubber sandals, a cotton blanket, a mosquito net, and a small towel (what we would refer to as a hand towel or dish towel).

The standard Vietnamese rest period was from about 11 am to 2 pm. During this time the guards rested and the POWs attempted to communicate from cell to cell. Some POWs would exercise by doing push ups or pacing the 2 or 3 steps to the end of their cell and back again. They would calculate how many steps back and forth would equal a mile. Some of them walked miles in a day; others ran in place. In the last two years the better diet made it possible for some to run ten or twenty miles a day and complete hundreds of sit-ups and push-ups. Some individuals pushed themselves to do over a thousand repetitions in a day. It helped them pass the time.

Normally, except to empty their waste bucket and to wash, prisoners were kept in their cells. In some cases prisoners were required to sit on their sleeping board or platform until the gong signaled they should go to sleep. In some cells, in some camps, a small wattage light bulb remained on twenty-four hours a day.

All of this describes what was a normal day for many POWs under normal circumstances. Normal was frequently interrupted. An example of this interruption would be the two POWs in one cell who were punished for not cooperating with interrogators. For ten weeks they were issued no toilet paper, no soap, no toothpaste, allowed only one bath a week, and given one pint of water per day for the two of them. There were many such interruptions in the life of an American POW in North Vietnam.

Senior ranking POWs were commonly isolated from other prisoners. They were usually housed in single cells and communicated only through various codes with other POWs. There were men in this group who spent four or five years in almost complete isolation. To combat the hours, days, and years of solitary confinement, men built imaginary houses, studied insects, recalled complex math formulas, or planned extravagant meals.

After the November 1970 Son Tay raid most of the POWs were moved to the prisons in Hanoi. From that point on few POWs were isolated. Most were housed in group cells. In some cases they were allowed more freedom of movement, at least within their compound.

Torture

Any discussion of the treatment of American POWs during the Vietnam War has to include the issue of torture. On their return in 1973 some POWs estimated that ninety-five percent of them had been tortured at some time, especially from 1965 through 1969. That torture varied in degree and duration.

Locking prisoners in ankle stocks or leg irons was very common. This might last for four or five days during which time the POW would never be released from

(Drawing used with permission of Mike McGrath.)

the stocks, urinating and defecating on their sleeping platform and themselves. It was common during this four or five day period not to be given any food or water, which helped keep down the mess (although weakness from starvation was the intended effect). If further punishment was to be given, the POW would be fed bread and water once a day after the initial period of starvation. Prisoners would try to clean the feces off themselves and their sleeping platform with their hands, unless those hands were cuffed or tied behind their back. Then they had to decide whether to use their limited water for drinking or cleaning their hands.

Release from the stocks might come periodically to use the waste bucket or to be interrogated. There were POWs who endured weeks and even months of this treatment. When kept in ankle stocks for longer periods of time they might be allowed out of the stocks ten minutes out of each twenty four hour day to clean their waste bucket. One POW was given eighty-five days in leg irons as a punishment.

The next step would often be beatings by the guards. They would enter the cell individually or in groups and punch and kick the prisoner. Ribs, teeth, and noses were often broken in these beatings. Sometimes clubs, rifle butts, or rifle cleaning rods were used. Flogging was prac-

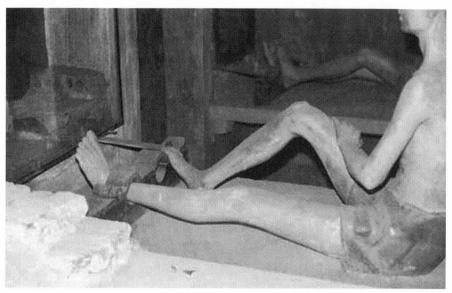

Photo from the Hanoi Hilton Museum. Lenient treatment meant only one leg in the stocks. (Courtesy of Renate Ecker.)

ticed by some guards. They used light bamboo rods or rubber whips cut
from old tires. There are accounts of POWs receiving 300 blows in one
session from such a whip. When being flogged the prisoner would be
stripped naked and forced face down on the floor. A guard would stand
on each hand and two others would hold each leg. One or two more
would handle the whips.

Beatings were part of the common practice of sleep deprivation. If
this took place in a torture room the prisoner would be forced to sit on a
stool or cement block about eight inches high. This position was designed to be physically uncomfortable. At least one POW was forced to
sit on a stool balanced on top of another stool. They would be punched
and screamed at every half hour or so to keep them awake or if they fell
off the stool. They would not even be allowed to leave the stool for
bowel movements. This would continue for four or five days until the
prisoner agreed to the demands of the guards. If the sleep deprivation
took place while the prisoner was in his cell he would be forced to stand
and bow every time a guard entered the cell. Guards would come into
the cell several times an hour. If the POW did not rise and bow he was
punched and kicked. Sleep deprivation was used as punishment or in an
attempt to get the prisoner to write propaganda statements. Some prisoners were able to endure this method of sleep deprivation for weeks.

Complete isolation was another common treatment. The extreme
form of this was to place a prisoner in a completely darkened cell. Ensur-
ing the cell was dark also meant there was no air circulation. The prisoner's clothing and/or his mosquito net might be removed. The cell was
usually not cleaned after the last prisoner had been there. Rats, bugs, and
spiders abounded in these cells. There would be nothing in the room except for a waste bucket. At times even this was removed. Food and
water were limited. If there was a waste bucket the prisoner might be allowed to empty it once a day – or not. In some cases the prisoners hands
would be tied behind his back and his ankles tied or put in cuffs. Some
were forced to eat with their hands tied behind their backs. That meant
getting down on the floor and licking their food from the bowl. Some
were thrown naked into a darkened cell with ankle stocks and their hands
tied behind their back. There would be only their latrine bucket, no bed
but the floor. Weakened from beatings and almost no food they could not

even stand. The cell would be so dark the only way they could find their latrine bucket was to crawl around until they bumped into it with their head, usually spilling some of the contents onto themselves in the process. This could, and often did, go on for weeks.

Senior POWs literally spent four and five years in isolation. Their only contact with other Americans came from the tap code or whispers through a small crack in a boarded up cell window.

If the prisoner was not cooperating by this time torture cuffs would be applied to their wrists. These were steel cuffs or manacles, locked by a key wrench. As long as the key was turned, the cuffs were ratcheted down tighter and tighter, causing instant and severe pain. They could be tightened right down to the bone. This would cause tearing and cutting of the wrists and quickly cut off the flow of blood to the hands. The hands would swell up and turn black. At times these cuffs were applied higher up on the arm.

The torture cuffs would be applied and the prisoner locked into the ankle stocks on his sleeping platform. With his arms cuffed behind him and ankles in stocks, the prisoner could not lie back down to sleep. He would have to remain upright, legs straight out before him. If he went to sleep and fell back on his arms the pain from the cuffs would wake him or the guards would come into the cell and beat him. The weight loss of the POWs meant little or no body fat, including their buttocks. Being forced into this position for long periods of time caused huge sores. To further complicate the matter, the prisoner would not be released to use his waste bucket. Some POWs remained in torture cuffs for more than a month. The cuffs might be removed twice a day to eat and use the waste bucket. The torture cuffs were frequently combined with the ropes treatment described later. Being in the torture cuffs for an extended time meant not being able to use your hands or arms for weeks or even months.

Being put into the ropes was one of the worst of the torture techniques used by the Vietnamese. A prisoner would have his ankles tied together and wrists tied or cuffed behind his back. His arms would then be tied together so they were touching from the elbows to the wrists. The method used to tie the arms together also shut off circulation in the arms and hands.

At this point a rope from the wrists might be tossed over a hook or beam in the ceiling and the prisoner hoisted off the floor, still with his arms behind his back. Done in a violent enough motion, this would dislocate the shoulders or break the arms. The prisoner might be stood on a chair with the rope leading to a beam and the chair kicked out from under him. Instead of tying the hands with ropes the torture cuffs might be used.

Another variation would be to place the prisoner's feet in ankle stocks, pass a rope from the wrists behind the back up over the head to the ankles, and pull the prisoner forward until his face was against his legs. POWs told of being forced into this position until their nose was pressing against their anus.

The position was also reversed. Placing the prisoner on his stomach, the guards would run a rope from the ankles to the prisoner's neck and pull him into a bow.

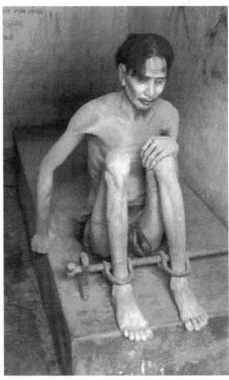

Another variation was to place the prisoner on his sleeping platform face down. The ankle stocks would be put in place, a rope passed from the wrists or elbows to a beam or hook, and the prisoner lifted off the sleeping platform by the rope. His feet were held in the stocks and the rest of his body was suspended in the air.

The following is a description of being put into the ropes by Robbie Risner, as told in the book *P.O.W.* by John Hubbell. After thirty-two days in stocks and on a starvation diet Lt. Col. Risner was released from the

When in this type of leg irons a POW had to remain sitting. The bar behind the ankles prevented any other position. Photo from the Hanoi Hilton Museum in Hanoi. (Courtesy of Renate Ecker.)

stocks, blindfolded, wrists tied behind his back, and thrown on the floor. "Tight half-hitches were applied to one arm, from the wrist to the shoulder. As each loop was strung, a guard stood on the arm and pulled the rope as tightly as he could. Then he took the rope a few inches up the arm and tied a new half-hitch ... The same thing was done with the other arm. Then the arms were pulled behind his back and tied together from the elbows to the shoulders." He "felt his right shoulder pull out of its socket, and he could feel the left shoulder trying to pull out ... Now his legs were tied in tight half-hitches from the ankles to just below the knees." His ankles were tied together, a rope attached to his ankles and then stretched behind his back and looped around his neck. The guards then pulled the rope tight to cause him to form an arch with his stomach on the floor and his head and ankles elevated. To keep from choking he could not allow his body to relax. Risner described the pain as "a living evil, writhing into every nerve ending." When he could not stop groaning with pain the guards punched him in the face. When the pain from the ropes and the beatings finally brought him to the point where he

(Drawing used with permission of Mike McGrath)

agreed to sign a statement of apology his hands could not function.

POWs with broken arms or legs were put into the ropes. Guards would twist or punch the broken limb while the prisoner was held in position. Some of the guards were very adept at relieving the pain just before a prisoner was about to pass out. Then they would continue. When the prisoner screamed, a rag would be stuffed in his mouth. The rags were never clean. At times the guards would use the same rags the POWs used to tie their sandals to their feet. Since clubs and rifle barrels were often used to push the rag into the mouth many prisoners had teeth broken in the process.

At first ropes were used for this torture, but they left very visible scars so the Vietnamese switched to webbing. The webbing straps would be carefully applied over shirt sleeves or pant legs so scars would be minimized. While tying the arms the torturer would actually stand on the prisoner's back to gain leverage in forcing the elbows and shoulders together. Sooner or later the ropes treatment broke the will of any prisoner. Usually the prisoner could not immediately write whatever statement the Vietnamese wanted because their hands and arms were swollen and numb. Especially from 1965 through 1969 there were POWs who were repeatedly subjected to the ropes treatment.

During the years 1965 through 1970 sixty-five percent of the POWs entered captivity. Those were also the years of the worst torture, in both frequency and severity. Torture was used by the North Vietnamese for a number of purposes. They wanted statements from pilots which they could use in their propaganda efforts against the United States. They tortured pilots to obtain "confessions" of their crimes in bombing hospitals and schools. They tortured prisoners to produce statements against the war and to find how they were communicating between their cells and with whom they were communicating. They tortured prisoners to find who the leaders were, to determine who was giving orders. They tortured prisoners to force them to meet with peace delegates and tortured them for not behaving as ordered during those meetings. They tortured prisoners who would not supply whatever information the interrogators were looking for. Many POWs were tortured in the summer of 1969 after two prisoners escaped from the Zoo Annex in Hanoi and were recaptured the next day. The most severe torture was experienced by those POWs who resisted all questioning and who attempted to provide leadership to their fellow captives. There were American POWs tortured to their death. Upon their return in 1973 the POWs reported they believed sixty-five of their fellow prisoners had died from torture or medical neglect or a combination of both.

Communication

The Vietnamese tried hard to prevent their American prisoners from communicating with one another. If they could keep the POWs isolated they had a better chance of obtaining written statements or recordings they could use for propaganda purposes. The American POWs developed various methods of communicating between cells, between separate compounds within camps, and between separate camps. There was even some communication back and forth between some of the prisoners and Washington, D.C. (This was accomplished through various codes in letters.)

The best known method of communicating was the tap code. The letter K was dropped from the alphabet and the remaining twenty five letters arranged in a 5 by 5 grid. The first series of taps gave the line across and the second series the line down. Three taps followed by two taps meant the letter M. The letter C took the place of K. The code was most commonly used to tap on the walls between cells. It could also be sent using a broom, by sneezing, coughing, and shuffling feet. Codes could be poked in paper and left where other POWs would find it.

This code was brought to Vietnam by a pilot who had attended a survival course where the instructor mentioned the method. The instructor had learned it from the British while a POW during World War II. He was not allowed to teach the code in classes as it was not part of the set curriculum but mentioned it in class, prompting some students to ask questions during a coffee break. One student remembered it when he was captured in the summer of 1965.

The tap code could also be used by flashing numbers with fingers. At times POWs could see each other by looking under the door. Other times they dumped water under their cell door so other prisoners could see their signals in the puddle's reflection. They also developed a method of shaping their hands into letters and symbols. At least one code developed by the POWs was so good the CIA could not decipher it when a version was given to them in 1973.

Written notes could be passed if some sort of paper and writing tools were available. These notes could be passed by hiding them in a bowl of rice when a prisoner was allowed to pick up his meal. Notes could be left in common areas such as a bath house or the tank where waste buckets were emptied. At times POWs were allowed to wash their clothing. They could put notes into pockets of other clothing hanging to dry. Messages were scratched on the bottom of food bowls. The POWs developed a code of arm and hand movements. Brushing the left arm with the right hand, wiping the brow with the left hand, scratching the head – all had meanings. Prisoners became so adept they could tap out messages while sweeping the compound with guards watching them.

A prisoner would pretend to be talking to a guard who spoke some English. He would use pig-Latin and actually be talking for the benefit of other POWs. A prisoner would pretend to be trying to talk to a guard who spoke no English. In reality he would be passing information to those prisoners in near-by cells. Some times the POWs could actually talk to each other in the early afternoon when the guards typically rested. A prisoner could put his drinking cup against the wall and talk to the next cell. A loud cough or thump on the wall ended all conversation or tapping. In some cases prisoners bored holes through the wall to the next cell. When they were caught they were often severely punished, especially prior to 1970.

Some POWs managed to get messages out in letters they were allowed to write to their families. Coded messages were sometimes received in letters from home. The idea for the raid on Son Tay evidently originated from the camp itself. Some of the POWs requested a rescue force. In another instance an escape attempt was coordinated with US forces but the attempt called off by the senior ranking POW.

When forced to record statements which were to be broadcast to other POWs, prisoners would use terms like "Horse Shit Minh" to let their fellow prisoners know they were being coerced. One of the most famous examples of prisoners getting their message across occurred when a POW blinked out the word "torture" while being filmed for propaganda purposes and the film was shown in the West.

Medical Care

Medical care provided to the POWs was minimal and often withheld for long periods of time as a means of persuasion. It is very probable that many of those prisoners who did not return died from injuries and illnesses the Vietnamese did not or could not treat. There were some cases of seriously injured POWs being sent to civilian hospitals in Hanoi for treatment. There were more cases of POWs in need of such treatment never receiving it.

Although medical care, when made available, was outdated and crude by standards the POWs were accustomed to, most of the time it was the same care as available to the Vietnamese themselves. The difference was that care was frequently and deliberately withheld and injuries often further aggravated as a means of torture.

Food

In the first year or so of Americans being held in North Vietnam they were fed three meals a day consisting of sliced bread, meat, and vegetables. Even so, some of the first POWs had meals so poor they became sick and quickly lost weight. From 1965 through 1970 the prisoners typically received two meals a day, the first about 10 am and the second about 4 pm. Meals included a bowl of watery soup made from the vegetable of the season: pumpkin, turnip, kohlrabi, or squash. A second bowl consisted of whatever vegetable the soup was made from fried in fat. Some days however, a meal consisted only of a handful of rice and a bowl of warm water. Often the rice was of poor quality and included gravel and grit. Many POWs formed the habit of swallowing the rice without chewing it to prevent damage to their teeth. When a prisoner was being punished or the guards were in a bad mood, the vegetables would not be washed of the human excrement applied in the fields. Dirt would be deliberately thrown on the food. The bowls of food would be left just outside the door of the cell to get cold and allow rats to help themselves. Prisoners told of setting down the moldy bread while they ate their soup only to have rats nibbling on it when they reached for it again. New prisoners often thought they were eating rye bread until they found the dark flecks were bugs or rat feces. It was not uncommon for the soup to contain pig feet, chicken heads, rotten fish, or chunks of fat with hide and hair attached.

Prisoners scheduled for early release would be fed three times a day with more food of better quality, including fresh bread. They were also allowed out of their cell so the sun would darken their obvious prison skin tone.

Special meals which included fruit and candy were commonly provided three or four times a year at holidays. It was also common for the Vietnamese to film the POWs eating those meals, usually in groups. There was no filming of meals the prisoners ate in their cells the remainder of the year.

In 1970 meals generally began to improve. A third meal was given to the POWs, usually a breakfast of toast and perhaps a small amount of milk. The quality of the soup improved with the addition of noodles and better vegetables. By 1972 food from packages was made available. This included vitamins, condensed milk, and fruit. These packages were either from the Red Cross or packages sent by relatives but never given to the prisoner to whom they were sent.

Mail

The first American held in North Vietnam was initially allowed to write two letters a week and received mail frequently. That practice ended as more POWs were captured. Typically, a prisoner might be allowed to write a letter about a year after he was first captured and might be given a letter some time in his second year of captivity. Letter writing was frequently a privilege which had to be earned. Earning the privilege meant writing some kind of propaganda statement, often after being tortured for refusing to write that statement. Allowing a prisoner to write home and giving a prisoner his mail from home were only done to benefit the Vietnamese. It was either a reward or a punishment. A prisoner might be given a letter at Christmas time with family photographs or news of a family death. The hope was that an already depressed POW would be that much more open to suggestions of better treatment if only they would write a statement. A letter might be shown to a POW but not actually given to him until he demonstrated a "correct attitude". Many letters sent from families in the states were received in North Vietnam, but most were not delivered.

If there was an average number of letters received by POWs it was probably two per year and they were commonly months old. Prior to 1970 some prisoners were never allowed to write or receive mail. Of about 500 packages sent to the POWs during two Christmas seasons early on, none were given to the prisoners and almost all were returned to the senders. In 1971 and 1972 prisoners were more likely to receive mail. Just before they were released in 1973, some prisoners received as many as twenty or thirty letters, some written as many as six years before. Again, the death of Ho Chi Minh and released POWs speaking publicly about torture seemed to mark a general improvement in treatment of POWs. After 1969 many prisoners received mail on a more regular basis. Still, at their release in 1973, ninety-five POWs had never received a letter from home and eighty had never written a letter that was actually mailed by the North Vietnamese. The group felt those most likely to be allowed to write and receive mail were those prisoners whose names were known to U.S. officials. A prisoner who had been listed as MIA most likely had not been allowed any mail privileges.

The Vietnamese used the Geneva Convention as their excuse for treatment of American prisoners of war. Since no war had been declared, they were not bound by the Geneva Convention. No declaration of war meant no prisoners of war. Their American captives were referred to as criminals.

Yet, by their own actions, they demonstrated their treatment of the POWs was wrong and they knew it. Prisoners were threatened before interviews with peace delegates not to mention how poorly they were treated. Those prisoners being released early were told if they talked about their treatment, the Vietnamese would release to the public the antiwar statements the prisoners had signed under torture. POWs being released early, and all the POWs at Operation Homecoming, were deliberately fattened up before release. In the months before their release they received medical care rarely experienced during their captivity. The Vietnamese kept a show camp where visitors were allowed to observe healthy-looking prisoners performing everyday tasks. Films were produced showing prisoners relaxing in groups or playing volleyball. At times they failed to cut all the scenes which showed the guards in the background threatening those prisoners. The Vietnamese "humane and lenient treatment" of the POWs was a sham and they knew it.

POWs held in South Vietnam and Cambodia as they are released at Loc Ninh mid-February 1973. (NARA photo)

POWs held in North Vietnam going through formal release at Gia Lam airport outside Hanoi February 1973. (NARA photo.)

Chapter Nine

North Vietnam—The Camps

There were fourteen established POW camps in North Vietnam. (A CIA study claimed nineteen known camps. It is not known whether they were referring only to camps in North Vietnam.) Twelve of the fourteen were in or near Hanoi. Many of them were known by more than one name, the result of references to sections within a prison compound. The most well known, the Hanoi Hilton, had fifteen sections within its walls, each referred to by a separate name. Some of these prison camps also held South Vietnamese and Laotian military prisoners and North Vietnamese civilians, including children. Some of the prisons had been built by the French; others were buildings modified to hold American POWs.

It was common for downed American pilots to be taken to the Hanoi Hilton when they were first captured. They would be questioned and later sent to Briar Patch or the Zoo. Later they might be returned to the Hilton. Frequent transfers to other camps or to compounds within the same camp were normal. After arriving at a prison camp for the first time, POWs would often receive a standard issue of supplies. This consisted of a set of red-striped pajamas, underwear, sandals, a cotton blanket or two, mosquito net, toothbrush, water jug, cup, soap, a towel, three pieces of toilet paper (paper bag consistency), a straw mat, and a waste bucket. The towel was the size of our kitchen towel. These supplies might all be issued at once, not issued until later, or only some of them issued. At times some of these items were removed as a form of punishment. The "pajamas" were the standard prison uniform consisting of a pair of light weight cotton pants and shirt. Later they were replaced by black or dark blue uniforms. These prison uniforms were standard clothing for the average Vietnamese. The term "pajamas" comes from the Western perception of this lightweight clothing being similar in appearance to pajamas worn at home.

Alcatraz

Alcatraz was opened at the end of October 1967 to hold eleven strong resisters the North Vietnamese wanted to separate from the other POWs in Hanoi. It was a ten minute drive but a separate reality from the Hanoi Hilton. The small compound, a former high security prison used by the French, had two buildings, one with three cells and one with ten cells. The cells were four by eight foot in size with a concrete pad for sleeping. They were dug into the ground which meant dirt walls and no windows. Tiny holes above the door and a small space below the door allowed in the only light and the only air. Tin roofs on the cells soaked up the heat in the summer and provided no insulation in the winter.

The prisoners were kept in their cells in the dark most of the time. Four times a day they were individually taken from their cell to empty their latrine bucket, wash, and get their two meals. From late afternoon until morning they were kept in leg irons. Some POWs learned to pick the locks and were able to remove the shackles during the night. The guards quickly tired of having to place the irons on each POW so they

The building with ten cells is the lighter colored building at the right. The three cells are to the left. (NARA photo)

would toss them in the cell and watch from the door to see that they were attached. Some POWs developed a technique of making the correct moves and sounds but not fully locking the shackles. When the guard left they could remove them and sleep more comfortably. Either way, picking the lock or not actually locking them, put the individual at great risk if they were discovered.

The guards tried to keep the eleven isolated from each other but the POWs used the tap code on the walls of their cells or its equivalent of coughs and sneezes while cleaning the compound. If caught trying to communicate with the others their leg irons would remain in place day and night. The standard punishment was ten days in leg irons. One POW at Alcatraz spent just under three months with his leg irons never being removed. Torture was the norm at Alcatraz. The prisoners were pushed to produce confessions or anti-war statements. They faced the ropes, beatings with rifle butts, and floggings. The isolation and torture at Alcatraz led to the death of one of the eleven.

In December 1969 most of the men were sent back to the Hilton. Three remained at Alcatraz until the end of May 1970.

Prisoners held here included: George Coker, Jeremiah Denton, Harry Jenkins, Sam Johnson, George McKnight, Jim Mulligan, Howard Rutledge, Robert Shumaker, Jim Stockdale, Ron Storz, and Nels Tanner. **Died:** Ron Storz

Bao Cao/Portholes

Bao Cao, or Portholes, was in the northern part of the panhandle of North Vietnam, in the area of Vinh. The camp held those POWs originally captured in South Vietnam and Laos. Most of them got to the camp in March of 1968. Within the camp, civilian prisoners were held in fifteen cells in a compound called Duc's Camp; enlisted prisoners were in the cells called Minh's Camp, and officers in a third section. Each building was separated from the others by 200 feet or more in a wooded area. The first American POW was kept in a two foot high cage his first four months at Bao Cao in the fall of 1967. He was chained all day except for a ten minute break to wash and use the latrine. It was here he met the first Americans he had seen in four years.

The civilians were kept in a 16' by 40' building with seven cells on one side and eight on the other. Each cell was 6' by 6' by 3' wide. Ankle stocks were in each cell with the locks outside. Prisoners whispered through the walls in this building. One of the civilians brought the officers their food and helped keep communication open. There were no latrine buckets in these cells and the guards were not always willing to let the prisoners out. Eventually they were given bamboo tubes to use for urination at night and then let out to empty them in the morning.

Each cell had wooden leg stocks and nothing more. Some were extremely small and isolated from the other buildings. Prisoners slept on thin mats on the wooden floor. They were given a mosquito net, a blanket, bowl, toothbrush, small towel, and the standard Vietnamese clothing. Meals of rice and watered-down vegetable soup were served twice a day. The vegetable soup, pumpkin or squash, was a welcome addition and many of the prisoners gained weight at Bao Cao. The standard routine was up at 6 am with meals at 10 am and 4 pm. Some could bathe every third day in the river, others only once a week. Prisoners were frequently kept in their leg stocks. Most were isolated from other POWs. Interrogation sessions of eighteen to twenty hours were common, often accompanied by beatings. Some of the cellblocks were dug below ground with only the thatched roof showing. These cells were different from the norm in that the walls and floors were constructed of regular boards. These buildings had eight cells, a straw/sod roof, and were surrounded by barbed wire. The name Portholes came from the round holes cut into the doors of these cells to allow ventilation. The camp opened in the fall of 1967 and was closed in the summer of 1968. One group left in early July and on 25 August the remaining forty or so left. Each individual carried their own gear roped up in a bundle and a twenty pound sack of rice for their meals on the trip. Some were sent to Farnsworth and others to Skid Row.

The name of the camp came from the phrase the prisoners were to use any time they wanted to address the guards. The phrase "bao cao," essentially meaning reporting for duty, was to be accompanied by a bow. In essence the prisoners were being made to salute the guards as if they were their superiors. This phrase was required in all the POW camps in North Vietnam but for the POWs transferred up from the South it was a new twist in their captivity, thus their name for the camp. Some POWs apparently used the terms "Closet" and "Telephone Booth" in reference to Bao Cao. These names probably came from the small cells. "Portholes" came from references to the small windows cut above the cell doors.

Prisoners held here included: John Anderson, Bruce Archer, Cloden Adkins, Candido Badua, William Baird, Art Balagot, Harvey Brande, Leonard Budd, Richard Burgess, Marc Cayer, Robert Chenoweth, Gary Daves, James DiBernardo, Carrol Flora, Ted Gostas, Robert Helle, Alex Henderson, Abel Kavanaugh, Michael Lenker, Edward W. Leonard Jr , Phil Manhard, Paul Montague, Lewis Meyer, Mike O'Connor, Robert Olsen, Russell Page, Ben Purcell, Don Rander, King Rayford, Alfonso Riate, Joe Rose, Thomas Rushton, Richard Spaulding, Larry Stark, Dennis Thompson, Floyd Thompson, Chuck Willis, John Young, Roy Ziegler, and at least 3 soldiers from the South Vietnamese Army. Robert Craner, Guy Gruters, and Lance Sijan were held here in January 1968 and then sent by truck to the Hilton. (In their book, *We Came to Help*, Diehl and Schwinn say they were held at Bao Cao 1970. They were actually at Farnsworth.)

Dennis Tellier was apparently held at Bao Cao in mid 1969. In April and May 1970 Daniel Hefel and Tom Kobashigawa were apparently held here. In August 1972 Thomas Mott, John Murphy, and William Thomas were apparently kept here. All of them seem to have been held at Bao Cao for a short period on their way to Hanoi.

Briar Patch

Briar Patch, in a mountain area about thirty-five miles west of Hanoi, was opened in August 1965. There were nine buildings, four cells in each, totally walled off from the other buildings with no electricity or running water. The prisoner diet led to malnutrition for POWs held there for an extended time. Ten prisoners were held here in the beginning and then bombing raids in the area led to the camp being closed in late September when they were sent to the Zoo. It was re-opened that December and held prisoners until February 1967. A few POWs were held here from February until July 1971.

The cells here were about 7' by 10' in size with bars on the windows and shutters that allowed in almost no light. During the winter months they were very cold. Two cotton blankets were the only protection against winter temperatures under forty degrees Fahrenheit. Most of the cells were two-man, but some had double bunks to hold four men with planks for sleeping. The windows and doors of each cell were situated to prevent the occupants from seeing anyone else in that set of cells. In the beginning of 1966 a bathing area was constructed using water drawn from a well. The prisoners got a bath every ten days, usually without soap. As in all the other camps, bathing was a privilege which was frequently withheld as a form of punishment. Food at Briar Patch was minimal. It was normal for a POW to discover the crunchy part of his meal was actually a roach he was eating in the dark.

Beatings and torture were common with prisoners being put in the ropes and cuffs on a regular basis as they were pressed by the North Vietnamese to produce confessions. Guards wore tennis shoes so they could move silently about outside the cells and catch POWs trying to communicate with each other. Loudspeakers were installed in the cell areas and three hours of propaganda blasted out each day..

By the summer of 1966 Briar Patch held about fifty-five prisoners. Sixteen of them were among those forced to participate in the Hanoi Parade that August where they were marched through downtown Hanoi while the crowd threw rocks and beat them. Beatings continued in the camp during 1966. A new twist was to force individuals to run around the compound barefoot and blindfolded. Sometimes pulled by a rope around the neck, they were purposefully run into objects. The two meals a day consisted of a handful of rice and a bowl of warm water. The windows were kept boarded over during the summer, making the cells extremely uncomfortable. Screams of those being tortured could be heard by others in the camp. Torture cuffs were regularly used on the POWs, followed by beatings with fists, clubs, and metal bars until they wrote some kind of confession. POWs were regularly put in the ropes, leg irons, and ratchet cuffs. Everyone in the camp was tortured that summer. For a period of time in late 1966 at least some, and probably all, of the prisoners were kept in cuffs twenty-four hours a day except to eat.

Four foot deep bomb shelters were dug in some cells and shelters dug into the sides of the hills near the camp. Each of these had a door installed and held two prisoners. For a short while drills were held in which some of the POWs were led from their cells to these hillside shelters. Both types of shelters were used as punishment, with some POWs spending a few days in the hillside holes and some spending a month in the holes in their cells. Some were placed in these holes in their cells with their hands cuffed behind their backs, giving them no way to ward off the bugs and mosquitoes that thrived in the damp. That same summer a version of barrage balloons was tethered around the camp.

Toward the end of 1966 conditions improved with some guard changes. Prisoners were allowed out of their cells, only one at a time, to clean up the area and work on a garden. At one point vitamin shots were given to at least some of the POWs, but the dates on the vials used were as much as ten years old. Briar Patch was closed in the beginning of February 1967 with half of the fifty plus POWs sent to the Zoo and the others to the Hilton. In February 1971 a few prisoners from Unity were held at Briar Patch along with a prisoner shot down that month over Laos. Those sent from Unity were also part of the small group originally captured in Laos. At times during their few months here they were put in a tunnel or underground room reached by ladders.

Dirty Bird

Dirty Bird held about thirty prisoners from 18 June until 25 October 1967. Its purpose seems to have been to prevent US air strikes on the nearby power plant in Hanoi. There were actually three buildings holding POWs. The first building was called Dirty Bird because of the coal dust and general debris. A month later a second building nearby was opened for prisoners which generally became known as Dirty Bird Annex or Dirty Bird West. For various reasons it was also called Army Post, Dog House, Foundry, and Power Plant. A third building, an old Chinese school, was added. Some referred to it as the School and some as Trolley Tracks. Since different prisoners were rotated in and out of the three sites it took a while to determine there were actually only three locations, even though they were right next to each other.

Both Dirty Bird and the Annex had eight larger-than-normal cells. The School had seven cells and at one point held just under 20 prisoners. All of the buildings and cells were filthy. The rooms used for cells had their windows blocked off with boards and pieces of tin so air movement was negligible. There were enough gaps, though, for the prisoners to watch the daily routine on the street outside. Prisoners were allowed out of their cells for longer periods of time than at most other camps. However, they were still isolated as much as possible from each other, frequently had to wear leg irons and cuffs, and the food was even lousier than at most other camps.

Individuals and groups were transferred into Dirty Bird and then out again. While there they were frequently moved around outside the compound to make sure the word got out that POWs were held in the area. In mid October two POWs escaped from Dirty Bird and floated down the Red River through the night before being caught. Due to that escape, or because the power plant was still a regular target of bombing raids, all three of the Dirty Bird compounds were closed down at the end of October 1967.

(NARA photo.)

Dogpatch
(approx 22 28 01 N 106 24 45 E)

Dogpatch was opened in mid-May of 1972 when 209 POWs were sent out of Unity in a sixteen truck convoy. The camp was 103 aerial miles north-west of Hanoi, very near the Chinese border. When they arrived after an uncomfortable one and a half day journey, the POWs found what seemed to be a newly built camp. There were about twelve concrete buildings used to house the prisoners, each about 30' by 50' in size. The standard configuration was two large cells and two small cells with ten foot high ceilings and bars in the windows. A few of the buildings were set up with eight small isolation cells. Each of the buildings held about twenty POWs in crowded conditions.

The buildings holding prisoners had a walled attached courtyard covered with bamboo lattice-work, itself covered with tar paper and leaves. The roof of each building was also camouflaged with tar and vines. Talking was allowed within individual buildings but communication was not allowed between buildings. Each was its own separate prison. The camp was situated on two small hills and enclosed by a seven foot high barbed wire fence on one half and a six foot high stone wall on the other. There were guard towers outside the perimeter and a large guard force with mortars and machine guns to keep the prisoners in line.

There were a number of unfinished buildings in the camp, enough to hold another 150 POWs was the guess. The buildings in use had been wired for electricity but there were no electrical outlets. Small kerosene lamps were used in the cells. The rooms were damp and dirty. Some reports say extra clothes and blankets were distributed. Meals usually included milk and some meat. Russian canned fish were part of the diet while they lasted. Water buffalo meat was purchased from the local villagers.

For the first time the POWs had some freedom from the constant observation by the guards. Within each building they were free to talk in the central hall. Their cells were unlocked about 7:00 in the morning and they were locked back up again about 5:00 in the afternoon. The exit doors were locked and the guards had to actually enter the building to observe the prisoners. When they first arrived the POWs were randomly assigned to buildings. On 25 October 1972 they were re-assigned according to their shoot-down dates. From October on they were not locked back up in their cells until 8:00 pm. No new captures were brought in to Dogpatch after the May move and they were too far north to be aware of the increased bombing around Hanoi. The October building assignments gave them the first hint that release was near. In the middle of January 1973 they were all trucked back to Hanoi.

Faith/Dan Hoi

Faith, also called Dan Hoi, was nine miles west of Hanoi. It was opened in July 1970 when prisoners from the Zoo and the Plantation were transferred from Hanoi in blacked out buses. At the same time all fifty-two POWs from Son Tay were transferred in.

Conditions at Faith came the closest to conforming to the Geneva Convention than at any other camp. There were six separate buildings designed to hold prisoners, although only four were used to house the 220 POWs brought in from the other camps. Each building was in its own separate compound enclosed by a high wall. Each had five large cells that held from ten to twenty prisoners. The rooms were newly white-washed and had separate beds. Food was available in sufficient quantities with bananas and oranges supplied every other day. Within each compound the prisoners could move about and freely visit with one another. Medical care was improved. The large numbers of prisoners and relaxed approach of the guards led to the first POW "university" being established, with classes held on subjects from auto mechanics to foreign languages.

They were still prisoners-of-war, however, and a few ended up in solitary confinement. The raid on Hope (Son Tay) on 21 November 1970 led to the entire camp population being sent back to the Hanoi Hilton on 24 November.

Farnsworth

Farnsworth, located about eighteen miles southwest of Hanoi, was opened in August 1968 when about twenty-five POWs were sent up from Bao Cao. The camp was evidently set up just to hold captives previously held in the South. When the group arrived from Bao Cao there were no prisoners in the camp. The enlisted were kept separate from the officers. There are references to Farnsworth as D-1 and Duong Ke. The geographical information in D-1 references fit the location of Farnsworth. NAM-POW includes the D-1 and Duong Ke nicknames in their information on Mountain Camp and does not list Farnsworth at all.

The compound consisted of at least eight concrete block buildings with red-tiled roofs. The area was surrounded by a barbed wire fence. There was a quarry off to the southwest and an airfield to the northwest. Several surface-to-air missile sites could be seen nearby.

The Drum, described as a building within a building (causing an echo-therefore the name Drum), was about 20' by 35' in size with its exterior painted yellow. Two of its rooms were for solitary confinement and the other two held as many as six POWs each. The Dispensary, of which one room was actually a dispensary, was about 20 by 70 feet. The rooms held ten to twelve POWs each. A 20' by 40' building called the Christmas building had six rooms. Its name came from the use of one room for a better than average meal and a Christmas celebration each year. Some of the rooms there were used for solitary confinement and others held six prisoners each. The Office was a building used for interrogation rooms and storage. An area called Death Row held three buildings, each about 10' by 12', with the third divided into two rooms. There are references to a building called the Long Building, but that may be another name for the Dispensary. There was a U-shaped building with seven cells that were apparently used for isolation. There were eight wells in the camp compound, each surrounded by bamboo screens. Prisoners bathed and washed clothes at the wells, probably one for each of the buildings holding POWs. Guards were posted at the perimeter gate, the entrance to each building, and throughout the compound. Bamboo fences separated the different areas in the camp.

At least one area of the camp had small isolation cells with no windows and the interiors painted black. This may have been the seven cells in the U-shaped building or those buildings called Death Row. Prisoners in these cells were supposed to sit on their bed, backs straight, throughout the entire day. They had two small meals a day and were allowed out of the cells only to use the latrine. The daily routine for prisoners in these cells meant getting up at 5 am and sitting on the bed with blankets folded until 7 am. At that point guards would take each individual from the cell to wash and empty their latrine bucket, then they had to sit on the bed until 11 am when the first meal was served. The small loaves of bread with the meals were new to the POWs from the South. They were allowed to lie on the bunks again during the two hour break all the guards took in the early afternoon, but had to sit on the beds again until the 4 pm meal, and again until 9 pm. Guards checked the cells a couple of times an hour. The only exercise allowed was the constant jumping up from the seated position on the bunk and bowing when the guards opened the small viewing port in the door of the cells. The torture and beatings here led to four attempted suicides among the POWs.

About twenty-five POWs from Bao Cao arrived at Farnsworth in late August 1968. On or about 25 December 1969 a group of about twelve POWs arrived from Camps 101/102. In April 1970 about twelve more POWs from the same area arrived. By the time the camp was closed at the end of 1970 there were about fifty prisoners at Farnsworth.

On their arrival the prisoners were given the standard "pajama" clothing of POW camps in North Vietnam. The daily schedule for the regular cells was to get up about 0500 and clean the rooms until 0530 when each building was allowed out to wash. At 0600 two cigarettes were given to each man and they were returned to their cells. Sometimes they were put to work sweeping their compound or pulling weeds in the garden. The morning meal was at 1100. Talking with prisoners other than those in your cell was forbidden. Supper was at 1630. A gong at 2100 was the signal to go to bed. For the first six months or so prisoners at Farnsworth underwent interrogation sessions and political lectures. They felt the camp was used for instruction purposes to train new interrogators.

In July of 1970 two or three slices of bread were given as a breakfast and the midday meal became lunch of a few slices of bread and a bowl of soup. Supper was the same as the noon meal. Around that same time period a doctor visited the camp every two weeks and provided treatment for at least some of the wounded in camp. In the fall doors and windows in the cells were allowed open more often.

On 25 November 1970, as a result of the Son Tay raid, the entire camp was sent by bus to the Plantation. They were blindfolded and had their hands tied for the trip.

Prisoners held here included: John Anderson, Bruce Archer, William Baird, Michael Benge, Harvey Brande, Leonard Budd, Richard Burgess, Robert Chenoweth, Luis Chirichigno, Lenard Daugherty, John Deering, James Dibernardo, Peter Drabic, Harry Ettmueller, Martin Frank, Ted Gostas, Ted Guy, Daniel Hefel, Robert Helle, Nathan Henry, James Holt, Thomas Horio, Juan Jacquez, Abel Kavanaugh, Gail Kerns, Michael Lenker, Stephen Leopold, Ed Leonard, Tom Kobashigawa, Cordine Mc-Murray, Don McPhail, Roger Miller, Paul Montague, Stanley Newell, James Nowicki, Michael O'Connor, John Parsels, Richard Perricone, Daniel Phillips, Don Rander, King Rayford, Alfonso Riate, Ronald Ridgeway, Joe Rose, David Sooter, Robert Tabb, Dennis Tellier, John Young, and Roy Ziegler.

Hanoi Hilton

The Hanoi Hilton was originally built by the French when they ruled Vietnam as a colonial power. Completed about 1900, the structure was designed to hold Vietnamese political prisoners. When the French left in 1954 the building was turned into a museum and then re-opened in 1964 to hold American prisoners-of-war. Americans were held there from August 1964 through March 1973. Today, what is left of the prison is again a museum.

The Hilton was a real prison, complete with guard towers, broken glass and barbed wire on the perimeter walls, and built-in ankle stocks in the cells. Located in central Hanoi, the Hilton became the headquarters of the prison system for American POWs in North Vietnam. Americans captured in the North were almost always taken first to the Hilton for their initial interrogation and then sent to the Zoo or Briar Patch. From 1965 through 1969 that initial interrogation almost always included brutal torture. Many prisoners sent to one of the other camps were periodically brought back to the Hilton for further questioning, which meant more torture.

In the beginning the Hilton had three main areas used for holding Americans. These areas were referred to as Heartbreak Hotel, Little Vegas, and New Guy Village. Half of the prison held Vietnamese, including women and children. At the end of 1970 these Vietnamese were moved out and all but a few of the American POWs in North Vietnam were moved into that section of the Hilton which then became known as Unity.

Heartbreak Hotel was where a prisoner was held when he was first brought into the prison. Each individual came into the prison expecting to be treated according to the rules of the Geneva Convention. They quickly learned that was not to be-thus the name Heartbreak Hotel. There were eight cells there, with the eighth being used as a wash area. Each cell was about seven by seven feet in size and held two cement sleeping platforms, one on each side. The sleeping platforms had built-in leg irons. Windows in the cells were boarded over. Prisoner interrogation at Heartbreak took place in a room known as Room 18, also called the Torture Room. This was a large room with sound-proofed walls and a hook in the ceiling. Prisoners were beaten for not answering questions beyond name, rank, and serial number and frequently found themselves being hung from the hook until their arms were pulled out of their sockets.

Little Vegas was opened up in January 1967 with the transfer of thirty-two prisoners from Briar Patch and twenty-two from the Zoo. It had sections known as the Cave, Desert Inn, Golden Nugget, the Mint, Riviera, Snake Pit, Stardust, and Thunderbird. The guards would throw garbage and feces in holes dug near the wells so the water the POWs had to bathe in was filthy. Cells in Little Vegas varied from one-man to four-man but even those were only nine by nine in size. The cells were set up with no door facing another to enforce a feeling of being alone. The Snake Pit was an area of one or more very small cells that were part of or near the area known as Golden Nugget.

Desert Inn had eight cells, the Golden Nugget three large cells, and the Mint three small cells considered high security holding areas. Thunderbird was the largest with fifteen cells. Stardust had seven cells used to hold those prisoners considered to have bad attitudes. The Cave was one small, dark cell. Calcutta, first used in 1970, was a very small and extremely dirty cell isolated from the others. It was only two or three feet by

(NARA photo.)

six feet in size and had almost no ventilation.

New captives were kept in four regular cells in New Guy Village. Here they were kept separate from one another and from older, more experienced, prisoners. The North Vietnamese hoped this feeling of isolation would make it easier to get the new arrivals to cooperate. Part of their attempt to get this cooperation was the Knobby Room. This was another torture room that got its name from the clumps of plaster on the wall that were meant to deaden the screams of those being "asked" to cooperate.

POWs would be moved from cell to cell and area to area within the Hilton with no apparent pattern. After 1965 they would frequently be moved to another camp and then maybe back again. Cells such as the Cave and Calcutta, and others used as punishment cells, were tucked away in corners or isolated in some other way. They were seldom, if ever, cleaned. A prisoner might be handcuffed and shackled for days and not even released to use the latrine bucket. The next prisoner placed in the cell had to live in that mess and probably added to it.

When Unity was created at the end of 1970 it had seven large cells that each held about fifty POWs in a 20' by 60' space. The prisoners slept on a large cement platform in the middle of each cell bay. Each of the seven areas was separated from the others by bamboo fences. One section, designated Zero, held the four senior ranking POWs and a group that had been captured in Laos (the Lulus-Legendary Union of Laotian Unfortunates, the name given to themselves by those POWs captured by the North Vietnamese in Laos.) In January 1971 Unity held just under 350 POWs. This included Thai Sgt. Chi Charn Harnavee and South Vietnamese pilot Nguyen Quoc Dat, called Max. Both were of tremendous help to the Americans.

In general, the move to Unity brought some improvements in both diet and treatment for the POWs. Some of them had a difficult time adjusting to living in crowded conditions with forty roommates instead of one or none. It was at Unity that life came to resemble in some ways the stereotypical view of a POW camp. University level classes were taught, books and movies were recited from memory or acted out, even dance lessons were given. However, even in Unity there were constant reminders of treatment in the earlier years. The senior POWs were brought into Unity but remained isolated. The guards became more lenient but there were instances of prisoners being beaten. Individuals were periodically removed from the group and placed in solitary confinement back in Heartbreak or sent to the Zoo or the Plantation. An attempt to hold church services in February 1971 led to guards with fixed bayonets marching into the cellblocks. Some prisoners spent over a month in leg irons as punishment. Five of the Lulus were sent to Briar Patch for five months. In March 1971 thirty-six POWs, whom the North Vietnamese considered to have poor attitudes, were sent to Skid Row. They were kept there until November of the same year. In May of 1972 about 200 of the prisoners at Unity were sent to Dogpatch. They were brought back in January 1973.

On 31 January 1973 the prisoners at Unity were told of the peace agreements. Cellblocks were re-arranged to house POWs by capture date. The senior ranking prisoners were allowed to mix with the general population. More food became available than some could eat. Between the middle of February and the end of March 1973 the POWs were released in separate groups. On 12 February over 100 former prisoners-of-war boarded American C-141s at Gia Lam airfield. On 29 March the last group of sixty-seven did the same.

Hope/Son Tay

Hope, more commonly known as Son Tay, was twenty miles northwest of Hanoi. Opened in May 1968 because of the lack of space in
camps in Hanoi, the most Hope ever held at one time was fifty-three
POWs, although sixty-five were held there at one time or another. The
first prisoners arrived from the Hilton on 24 May 68, with more arriving in
July and November. Hope was a miserable place-filthy cells with no ventilation, rats everywhere, terrible food, and little medical care. The improvement for most of the prisoners was the fact they were housed in
larger cells with as many as ten to a cell.

No work had been done on the deteriorated buildings prior to the arrival of the first POWs. Sections of the small camp became known as the
Beer Hall, the Cat House, the Opium Den, and the Stag Bar. The Opium
Den had four three-man cells. The Oven was a punishment cell under one
of the guard towers. It was too small for a person to stand up in and became extremely hot during the day and very cold at night. One POW
spent two months in the Oven. Some called this punishment cell the Tank.
Some torture was carried out by the guards in their effort to produce confessions and tapes, but the majority of the prisoners were not tortured.

In the last months of 1969, as in the other camps, the boards were removed from the cell windows and some walls were taken down. Aerial
photography showed two newly constructed buildings in December 1969.
In early 1970 the quality of the food improved and some packages from
home were handed out. Some new buildings were constructed and a new
well dug, much of the work being done by the POWs. They used their
tools to pass information to other buildings with the tap code. In the summer of 1970 the well dried up, so much so it was used as a punishment
cell. Flooding from the near-by Song Con river was causing problems.
The camp was closed on 14 July 1970 and the entire group transferred by
truck to Faith.

Prisoners at Son Tay managed to arrange objects in their courtyard to
spell out a detailed request for a rescue. Reconnaissance aircraft spotted
their message. The camp, deep inside North Vietnam, was raided by an
American force in November 1970.

(A list of prisoners held here appears in Appendix I of the book *The
Raid-The Son Tay Prison Rescue Mission* by Benjamin F. Schemmer.
Rather than list them here I encourage you to read the book.)

Mountain Camp

On 12 December 1971 nine POWs from Skid Row were sent to a small camp about fifty miles north of Hanoi. On leaving Skid Row they were blindfolded and put in cages mounted on the back of a jeep. Prisoners at Mountain Camp were kept in individual cells and allowed outside only in the small walled-in area attached to each cell. One building had five cells and another had four. Although they were kept isolated, each 10' by 10' cell had a table, a stool, a straw mattress on a bed, and a latrine. The latrine had a cement sit-down toilet and a small tub which held the water they used to flush the toilet or pour over themselves for a shower. The area attached to each cell was of concrete and had barbed wire woven across the top. Prisoners were allowed out most days in their respective "veranda" but the guards only allowed one prisoner out at a time. Three meals a day were served. One of the nine December 1971 arrivals escaped for a few days in March of 1972.

The entire compound was enclosed by a nine foot high fence of bamboo covered in various plants. In July 1972 the barbed wire over each cell's exercise area was covered with vines, the roof and walls of the two cell buildings were painted with tar and kerosene, and trees were planted around the cellblocks-all apparent efforts to camouflage the camp. There was a separate building for the guards' quarters and two guard towers.

In October of 1972 the food improved and the American prisoners were allowed to eat as a group (except for Keesee). The two German volunteer nurses reported being asked to sign a document listing the food provided for each meal. One sick POW was given special attention to improve his health. Prisoners were allowed to work in a small garden within the camp walls. The camp was closed on 28 January 1973 when

Mountain Camp cellblocks
as drawn by Eugene Weaver

all the POWs were transferred to the Hanoi Hilton. The Germans, Diehl and Schwinn, were sent to the Hilton separately after the American POWs and kept isolated for their first ten days there. Keesee was also held separately from other Americans at the Hilton.

Prisoners held here included: Bernhard Diehl, Ted Gostas, Bobby Jo Keesee, Philip Manhard, Ben Purcell, Donald Rander, Monika Schwinn, Eugene Weaver, and Charles Willis. Rander and Willis shared one cell and one was used by the guards to cook the prisoner's meals. It is not known if any POWs were held at Mountain Camp prior to December 1971 but the lack of evidence would suggest not. Keesee had stolen a plane in Thailand in September of 1970 and ran out of gas over North Vietnam.

Plantation

Plantation was opened in early June 1967. It was a two acre complex that had been a government official's residence under the French, just across the street from Alcatraz. The first eight POWs sent from the Hilton actually did some of the work cleaning and repairing the compound. The camp was also called the Citadel, Country Club, Funny Farm, and Holiday Inn. Sections within Plantation were dubbed Corn Crib, Gun Shed, Movie House, the Show Room, and the Warehouse.

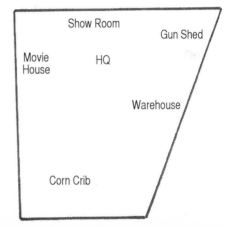

Along with serving a need to house the growing POW population, Plantation was set up to serve as a show camp where foreign press and peace delegations could see firsthand the "humane and lenient treatment" given to the prisoners.

The main house on the estate was used as guard quarters and offices and as the interrogation center. The POWs were housed in various buildings that had been the servants' quarters. The Warehouse was the largest and held fifteen cells. One of its cells had no door - the occupant had to crawl through a window. The Gun Shed had seven cells, the Corn Crib three cells, and one cell was in the Movie House. The Show Room had three cells and

(NARA photo.)

its purpose was defined by its name. These were the cells the visiting media saw and of course were most like those required under the Geneva Convention. These visitors were never taken to see prisoners being held in solitary confinement in the Corn Crib. The cellblocks had all been created by remodeling various rooms in the buildings. All cell windows were boarded over. Cells varied in size to hold from one to five to fifteen POWs. At least some of them had speakers over which Radio Hanoi was broadcast daily. As with most camps, prisoners were transferred in and out of Plantation on a regular basis, and from cell to cell within the compound. By January 1968 Plantation held about fifty-two POWs.

Even though a kitchen and a five-stall bath house were built, Plantation had a constant problem with its water supply. Prisoners received the standard two meals a day but at one point they ate nothing but soup for three straight months. The cells outside the Show Room were more standard. A few were used to isolate some prisoners for months. One of these had its only light bulb removed, but the bugs and rats didn't seem to mind and kept any occupant company during his extended stay. Outside the Show Room the camp was like all the others. There was even an escape in the summer of 1967.

The camp was also used during the summer of 1967 to film a propaganda movie that appeared in East Germany and the US. Media interviews were frequently conducted and US anti-war activists visited with POWs. Some of the prisoners paid a heavy price for not cooperating with these propaganda efforts.

Many of the POWs held here were recent captures who had not been exposed to the resistance found in other camps. They did not have obvious torture scars that would ruin the many photo opportunities given to the visiting press. The Vietnamese attempted to get these new arrivals to cooperate with confessions and positive letters home. A new POW would be told everyone was cooperating. He would be shown some of the better examples, not knowing the writer had been tortured. However, there were some hard line resisters brought into camp who managed to set up a chain of command and regular communication among the POW population. Some of them were beaten and whipped for these activities and eventually sent to other camps.

In February and August of 1968 two groups of three POWs each were released from Plantation to American peace activists. By that time about fifty prisoners were held there. That summer some of the more difficult prisoners were sent elsewhere.   At Christmas the POWs were given a special meal with all of them gathered together. The whole event was filmed as propaganda, but the prisoners managed to exchange information about names, conditions, codes, and orders from the senior ranking POWs in other camps. In August 1969 three more prisoners were released. In December many of the prisoners were transferred to the Hilton or elsewhere. In July 1970 Plantation was shut down. As a result of the Son Tay raid the Southern captives held at Farnsworth were moved into Plantation in December 1970. The Kushner Group arrived in the spring of 1971 and in July the Lulus were brought in from Briar Patch. For prisoners previously held in the primitive camps in the South and Laos, the Plantation was a drastic improvement. At that time about seventy POWs were held at Plantation. They were able to bathe each day and allowed exercise, but only one cell at a time. Classes were held each morning and they were pressured to write letters to peace organizations. Except for Sunday they had three meals a day. At one point some prisoners were required to hand-roll coal balls to be used in the kitchen.

By the summer of 1972 there were about eighty prisoners there. In late December 1972 and early January 1973 the POWs were sent to the Hilton and Plantation was closed again. On 20 January it was re-opened to hold those prisoners scheduled to leave in the third group, released on 14 Mar 1973.

Rock Pile

Rock Pile was thirty miles south of Hanoi. It was also known as Camp B and Stonewall. Rock Pile held prisoners from June of 1971 to January 1973. Isolated here were fourteen prisoners captured in South Vietnam and Laos, two of them US military and the rest civilian, including three Filipinos and one Canadian. They had been transferred from Skid Row to make room for POWs sent there from Unity. When they arrived at Rock Pile, after the four day march from Skid Row, they concluded it had been built or modified just for them. There was a sixteen foot wall surrounding the camp with a gate in one wall. The prisoners were kept in one large building inside the walled-in compound. The entire compound measured about 60 by 120 feet. The prisoners were kept in two cells, sleeping on rice mats on the raised sleeping platforms. Their clothes were rolled up each night and used as pillows. Three men slept on one side of the cell, four on the other. Four men could not fit easily so they alternated that fourth man. In each cell area there was an almost unheard of separate room for meals with a table and stools and a latrine. In the beginning the prisoners were allowed into the compound area twice

(NARA photo)

daily for exercise where they could play volleyball. They received much better medical care than any of them had experienced prior to their arrival at Rock Pile. Breakfast was French bread and sugar, the evening meal bread and boiled vegetables. Those conditions changed in October 1971.

After the October 1971 escape (and recapture) of three of the prisoners none of them were allowed outside for a year. Their food and medical care declined. No mail was sent or delivered. In December of 1971 they complained loudly to the camp commander and conditions improved but they still could not use their outside area. With all that time inside they began classes in algebra and French and put on a comedy play. After October 1972 they were again allowed to spend time outside. Fruit was included in their diet and the daily cigarette ration was increased. On 29 January 1973 they were told of the peace agreement and shortly after sent to the Hanoi Hilton where they continued to be separated from those captured in North Vietnam until their release on 5 March. Both Rock Pile and Mountain Camp were unusual in that they held small numbers of prisoners who had originally been captured in the South. Both camps were opened in 1971 and kept their prisoners until the end in January 1973.

The two military personnel held here were Frank Cius and Floyd Thompson. The civilians were Cloden Adkins, Candido Badua, Art Balagot, Marc Cayer, Gary Daves, Alex Henderson, Lewis Meyer, Robert Olsen, Russell Page, Tom Rushton, Richard Spaulding, and Larry Stark. (Candido Badua refers to Frank Cius as Frank Sears in his information found at www.badua.net).

Skid Row/K-77

Skid Row, also called K-77, was six miles southwest of Hanoi. It was named for the dirty and rundown condition of the buildings. The camp was enclosed by a fourteen foot high wall with barbed wire on top. One building housed the POWs, one the guards, the third was the camp kitchen, and the fourth was for the camp commander. Prisoners were held here from July 1968 through January 1972. Those who arrived in July of 1968 reported twenty-four US prisoners and fifty-six other nationalities already at Skid Row. POWs who would not cooperate at the Hanoi Hilton were sent to Skid Row. POWs captured in South Vietnam and Laos were also held here from July 1968 to June 1971. The main building housing prisoners was either an old monastery, with the former monks' cells now holding the POWs, or an old French penitentiary. There was at least one other building that held eight cells and a building with interrogation rooms. The main building held two rows of eighteen cells each. Each cell door had only a small opening which was covered with bars and a shutter on the outside. Each cell was about six by six feet in size with planks for beds. The cells had no windows and at least some of them had kerosene lamps. The building was concrete and the cell walls whitewashed. Between each cell holding a single US prisoner was a cell holding a Vietnamese or Laotian prisoner. Each prisoner was separately allowed out of his cell for a few minutes each day to wash and empty his latrine bucket. They were given two cigarettes a day (sometimes four), shaved three times a month (everyone using the same razor) and had their hair cut once a month. The food was better than what the POWs captured in the South had experienced, yet POWs transferred from Hanoi considered the food to be inadequate compared to what they had been eating. When the Paris peace talks began in January 1969 a breakfast of bread, sugar, and warm water was served every day but Sunday. Bread was available even though it usually contained bugs, small stones, and rat feces. Dysentery and a skin fungus were problems here. Interrogations continued, the prisoners were beaten, and leg stocks were used. However, overall the treatment was not as bad as any of them had experienced prior to coming to Skid Row.

In September 1969 at least the civilians from the South were put in a building of six four-man cells but still kept isolated from other cells. The morning meal was a small loaf of bread and a lump of sugar, the noon meal usually a bowl of soup and sometimes a cup of tea. There was an evening meal also. During the month of January 1970, fifty of the meals were boiled cabbage, bread, and hot water (two cups with each meal). That was all the water allowed for the prisoners each day.

In late 1969 the prisoners started receiving a one-page newsletter with the news from Radio Hanoi. Each page of this newspaper had the numbers 77 stamped on it, thus the name K-77. Loudspeakers broadcast Radio Hanoi on Sunday.

In March 1971 thirty-six POWs from Unity were sent to Skid Row and kept there until November. The guards at Unity considered them trouble makers and wanted them removed from the general population for a while. On 21 June fourteen POWs originally sent to Skid Row from Bao Cao were sent to the Rock Pile. In September twenty-one POWs were transferred from Hanoi to Skid Row and then returned to Hanoi in November. For a few weeks during December, small groups of prisoners from Unity were sent to Skid Row. The rest of the southern POWs were sent to Mountain Camp at the end of 1971 and Skid Row was apparently closed.

Some of the South Vietnamese POWs held at Skid Row told of seeing US prisoners they described as "walking skeletons." They also told of Americans passing them articles from Christmas packages and reported one US prisoner died of snake bite when a snake got in his cell.

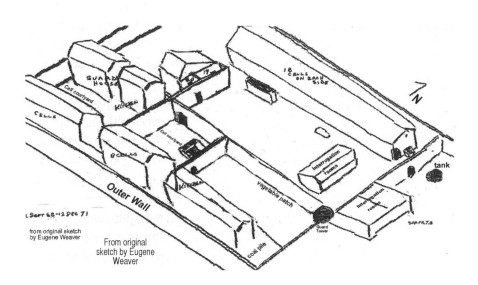

From original sketch by Eugene Weaver

There was an escape from Skid Row in December of 1969 when a prisoner actually made it into Hanoi trying to get to the French consulate. He was captured and sent back.

POWs transferred here from the south included Cloden Adkins, Candido Badua, Art Balagot, Marc Cayer, Gary Daves, Bernhard Diehl, Theodore Gostas, Alex Henderson, Lewis Meyer, Robert Olsen, Russell Page, Ben Purcell, Don Rander, Tom Rushton, Richard Spaulding, Larry Stark, Monika Schwinn, Dennis Thompson, Floyd Thompson, Gene Weaver, and Charles Willis. The two West Germans, Bernard Diehl and Monika Schwinn, were kept isolated from the others and from each other during the eighteen months they were at Skid Row.

Zoo

Opened in August 1965, the Zoo was on the southern outskirts of Hanoi in an old French film studio surrounded by an eight foot high wall. Along with the Hilton it became a major holding camp for POWs. Fourteen buildings were remodeled to hold prisoners with bars put in the windows and light switches moved outside the doors. The buildings had not been used for years and were filthy. In some of the newly-created cells brick supports were built to support the bed planks. Others had only the floor for a bed. Some cells had a light bulb glowing day and night; others had no light at all. A loudspeaker system was installed to broadcast the Voice of Vietnam at a high volume for a couple of hours a day. In the middle of the compound was an old swimming pool the guards used to raise fish and dispose of their garbage. Farm animals wandered around the whole area.

Walls were constructed around individual buildings to create separate compounds to hold prisoners. The Auditorium had a single punishment cell full of cobwebs and bugs. It was kept so dark any occupant could not see his hand in front of his face. The Outhouse was another punishment cell. There were no windows so it was extremely hot in the summer and retained the cold in the winter. A prisoner isolated there got one bowl of rice and two cups of dirty water each day. Since anyone held there was often in leg irons and handcuffs it was difficult to use the latrine bucket. The cell was never cleaned-thus its name. The Gatehouse was a long concrete building near the entrance to the Zoo. Cells there were dark, dirty, and hot. There was no air movement and prisoners often had no mosquito nets. The Barn had seven cells and the Pool Hall ten. Cells in the Barn initially had no beds at all until saw horses were brought in and wooden planks placed across them for sleeping. There were no windows with the only ventilation coming from three holes high on both the front and back wall. The Pool Hall cells were two-man with pallets for beds and no windows. The wooden doors had a smaller door inset that was used to pass the water bottles in and out. There was also the Stable and the Pigsty, which originally had two prisoners in each of its three cells and by 1970 held four to six in each cell. The hut, also called the Gym, was another small building used for solitary confinement.

In the spring of 1966 there were forty-five POWs at the Zoo and a year later about 120. Treatment was rough. The punishment cells were dark and hot, with summer temperatures frequently over 100 degrees. Prisoners were kept in these cells for three weeks at a stretch. During that time they were likely to have no mosquito net, their ankles in stocks, and their hands tied behind their back. They might be let out once a day to clean their latrine bucket. Some POWs were kept in solitary most of their time at the Zoo. Many were tortured to sign statements or to have their interviews with foreign press delegates filmed. Confessions were printed in the Vietnam Courier, an English language publication in Hanoi. There was actually a torture machine used at the Zoo to get those confessions, with ropes and pulleys to contort a prisoner's body. Thirty-six POWs from the Zoo were forced to march in the Hanoi Parade that August. In late 1966 and late summer 1967 many of the prisoners were tortured. It was during this time several Cubans severely tortured two groups of ten POWs. One prisoner was given three hundred lashes in a three-day period with a whip made from a tire. During that time his wounds were left untreated and his mosquito net was taken away. At least one prisoner died from his treatment at the hand of the Cubans.

During 1967 the cells were commonly searched twice a day. Prisoners had to wear their long pajama uniforms and sit on the bed during the day while listening to Radio Hanoi. They were beaten for not folding their blankets correctly. Cell doors and windows had any cracks sealed. Sitting in hot clothing in the extreme heat caused many prisoners to break out in boils. One counted over 200 on himself. Small hand fans were given out to help cope with the heat. In the winter it was the opposite with the cells being cold and no extra clothing or blankets supplied. Some POWs wore their pajama bottoms upside down so they could close the drawstring and keep their feet warmer.

In early 1969 conditions improved at the Zoo for a short time. Daily bathing was allowed for most and the food included some meat. In May an escape attempt from the neighboring Zoo Annex ended that improvement. Cells were sealed up even tighter. For six weeks prisoners were severely beaten, whipped, and even given electrical shocks. One POW endured over 300 lashes and another over 700. One of the escapees died from the torture. During the fall conditions improved again. By 1970 the beatings and torture at the Zoo had for the most part disappeared, although not completely. That summer the prisoners were allowed to play basketball and volleyball and were given chess and checker sets. Some Bibles were even handed out. They were allowed to move about within their separate compounds and allowed to bathe when they wanted. There were still interrogation sessions and staged propaganda photos taken but for the majority of the POWs treatment was much better than before.

On 26 December 1970, as a result of the Son Tay raid, the Zoo was closed and the sixty to seventy prisoners still held there transferred to the Hilton. In September 1971 about fifty POWs were sent back to the Zoo. From then until release it was used primarily to house new shoot-downs and for visiting peace delegations. During the summer and fall of 1972 the camp was cleaned up and some areas painted to help impress those delegations. In September of 1972 three POWs at the Zoo were released. At various times some prisoners were transferred over from Unity for a while and then sent back. On the 28th and 29th of March 1973 the last POWs left the Zoo.

The Zoo Annex, sharing a perimeter wall with the Zoo, was opened in October 1967. Four or five buildings were each divided into two cell areas. The cells were about 20' by 20' in size and held from four to ten prisoners each. Each cell area had a squat toilet. The buildings were centered around a pond called Lake Fester. The Annex eventually held just over sixty POWs.

The Annex seems to have been created as a place to keep junior officers. They were generally treated better than at the Zoo but were also pressured to write statements or make tape recordings. POWs were regularly allowed out of their cells to work in a garden or clean up the grounds. In May of 1969 this treatment changed with the escape of two POWs from the Annex. Some prisoners were tortured and put on half rations while wearing leg irons. Others were transferred to the Hilton for more questioning and torture.

At the end of August 1970 the sixty-one POWs at the Annex were transferred to Faith.

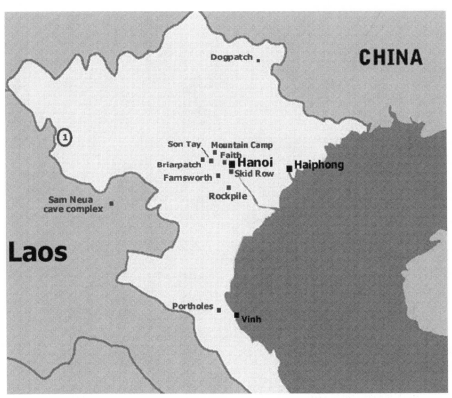

Map of Camps in North Vietnam. The circled 1 designates the area where Ernie Brace was first held. Map created using Google Earth®

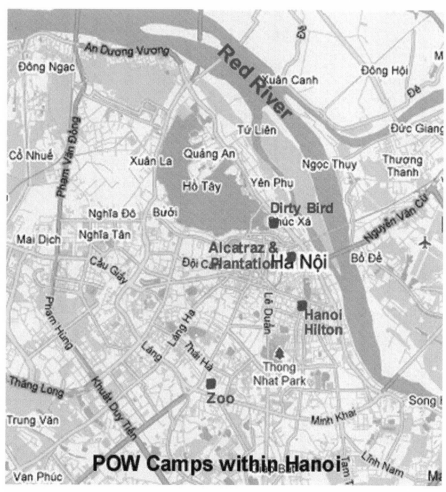

Map created using Google Earth®

Part III

Chapter Ten

Conditions in Laos

Prisoners of war held in Laos had three chances for survival. They could escape (3); they could be released early by their captors (28); or they could be sent on to camps in North Vietnam (10). Individuals not in one of these three categories simply disappeared. Only eleven POWs captured in Laos were returned alive in 1973, and these were the eleven sent to camps in North Vietnam (ten were American and one Canadian). North Vietnamese soldiers talked about twenty-four ways they could die while traversing the Ho Chi Minh Trail, much of which was in Laos. The twenty-four ways included tigers, snakes, floods, malaria, and dysentery. Those were the risks for healthy troops with every effort made to feed and house them. How were prisoners supposed to survive those conditions?

Perhaps the only Red Cross visit of the war occurred in Laos in 1961. Eight Americans had been captured in early 1961 and held under miserable conditions for a year and a half. Only four survived. At one point they were staked all night on their backs in the rain. Being placed in a cell did little to improve their condition. Their food was rice and weeds. They were kept in a dark cell except for a morning bath in a stream. While bathing they would pick leaves to eat. The guards were cruel and abusive. One American was killed when he refused to obey the guards. Six POWs were locked side-by-side in heavy ankle stocks for twelve hours at a time. They were transferred to a different prison for the Red Cross visit. During those few days they were housed in clean, sunlit cells with no stocks. They were given blankets and fed well. When the Red Cross inspection team left, the POWs were sent right back to the camp with the stocks and darkened cells. By the time of their release, one American had been killed, one starved to death, and two others simply never seen again.

Three more Americans were known to have been captured between

1963 and 1966. Within a few days of his capture one of them was tied
upside down to a tree and beaten, dragged behind a water buffalo, and
had an ants' nest jammed on his head. Guards shot at the prisoners for
entertainment. Food and water were scarce. All three eventually escaped, but only one made it back alive.

Captured in Laos in 1965, Ernie Brace was kept in various bamboo
cages for three years. His hands and feet were tied and a rope fixed
around his neck and then to a stake outside the cage. During the day his
hands and feet were freed and some slack allowed in the neck rope. The
cage was not large enough for him to stand. He was usually allowed out
twice a day to use the latrine. About every six weeks he was allowed to
bathe and wash his clothes. His food was mostly rice. Tied as he was at
night he could do little to escape the rats that crawled over him looking
for food and the snakes that came looking for the rats. Brace was held
with Thai Sergeant Chi Charn Harnavee but only caught a quick glimpse
of him a few times during the three years they were held in Laos.

After one escape attempt, his legs and neck were placed in stocks in
his cage. Another escape attempt got him buried up to his neck for a
week. Some guards treated him well, even providing him with necessary
medicine for various fungus problems. Other guards allowed him to almost die from neglect. He was allowed to write one letter in that three
year period in Laos, but the letter was never delivered.

During the war US officials believed American POWs were being
held in a cave complex at Sam Neua in northern Laos near the Vietnamese border. Numbers ranged from two to twenty. Various sources
would bring back pieces of information about who the POWs were and
how they were being treated. At one point some of them may have been
rescued or they may have escaped. No concrete information could be obtained because this was also a large base area. Radio intercepts during
the war mentioned POWs being killed by grenades thrown into a cave
somewhere in Laos. In 1993 a reliable Vietnamese source mentioned that
ten POWs held in a cave in Laos had escaped late in the war, were recaptured, and executed using grenades. An American flying for the CIA was
captured in May of 1973 and held in a cave complex near Sam Neua. He
described the complex as having two levels and holding almost 300 Laotian prisoners at that time.

Of the over 300 American POWs missing in Laos only ten returned in Operation Homecoming in 1973. All of them were captured by North Vietnamese troops in Laos, not Laotian troops. These ten (plus one Canadian) were sent from Laos to POW camps in North Vietnam. They called themselves the Lulus – Legendary Union of Laotian Unfortunates. The whole time they were in North Vietnam they were kept separate from other American POWs and were never allowed to write letters. In the summer of 1969 the first of the Lulus were moved to Hanoi and kept in the Vegas section of the Hilton. When Unity was opened they were moved there and kept isolated with the senior officers in what was called Building Zero. In February 1971 they were moved to Briar Patch and in July back to the Gun Shed at Plantation. Finally, they were moved back to the Vegas section of the Hilton and released on 28 March 1973. Even while in Unity they were separated from the other Americans.

It was through Laos that prisoners captured in the northern provinces of South Vietnam were taken north, eventually to Hanoi. Many captured in Hue made this journey on foot from the coast, across South Vietnam, through Laos on branches of the Ho Chi Minh trail, and then by truck to Portholes near Vinh. Many who started that journey never made it. Moving through Laos was very difficult, not only because of the terrain but also because of constant bombing raids. Those individuals who were not healthy enough to keep up were executed. In one group being moved north, a POW was sick and constantly lagging behind. At one point the leader of the group told a guard to shoot him if he did not immediately get up and start walking. This warning was not given to the POW. It was said in Vietnamese to the guard only. Another POW could speak Vietnamese and translated for the man on the ground. Most POWs would not have been so lucky.

Radio intercepts of units guarding the Ho Chi Minh Trail in Laos give proof that when those units took heavy casualties during bombing raids they sometimes executed POWs in retribution.

The LULUs: Henry Bedinger, Ernie Brace, Jack Butcher, Norbert Gotner, Ted Guy, Ed Leonard, Stephen Long, Sam Mattix, Lloyd Oppel (Canadian), Charles Reese, and Walter Stischer.

Chapter Eleven

Conditions in Cambodia

Conditions in camps in Cambodia were the same as camps across the border in Vietnam. Camps 101 and 102 were in Cambodia. Camp 102 was part of a VC base camp so at times the prisoners had better than average medical care but the food was no better than at other camps. When not near a base camp, medical care was almost non-existent. The prisoners were kept in bamboo cages, some with wooden stocks for their feet. Other times they were chained by their ankles. In one case, six POWs were kept in a five by ten foot cage.

Camp Delta was inside Cambodia. Here the POWs slept chained in the open in hammocks. The jungle was so thick they seldom saw each other even though they were only thirty feet apart. Camp Echo was most likely in Cambodia. At Echo the POWs lived in cages set below ground level. As a result Echo was also called Monkey Cages. Food was scarce so rats were on the menu. Monsoon rains turned the camp to mud. Anemia, beri beri, and dysentery added to the misery.

A French journalist, Yves-Michel Dumond, was captured in April 1972 with Albert Carlson and held in Cambodia. He escaped for two days in May. For that he was placed in a hole that was covered with logs and mud. For six weeks he was held in that small hole with his legs chained, even though the North Vietnamese knew they were going to release him. (He was released in July 1972.)

In 1972 David Baker, Albert Carlson, Johnnie Ray, Mark Smith, Ken Wallingford, James Walsh, and George Wanat were held just across the Cambodian border near Snuol. Baker was shot down over Cambodia and the others were captured in the Loc Ninh area of South Vietnam. In this camp they were held in bamboo cages, in at least some cases two to a cage. They slept in hammocks but were chained to the cages. Their three meals a day were rice with tiny portions of meat and vegetable. They were sent back across the border for release at Loc Ninh on 12 February 1973. Released at Loc Ninh were Keith Albert, David Baker, Norm Brooken, Albert Carlson, Frederick Crowson, John Dunn, John Fritz, Gary Guggenberger, William Hardy, James Hestand, Bobby Johnson, Michael Kjome, James Newingham, Daniel Maslowski, Felix Neco-Quinones, Douglas Ramsey, Johnnie Ray, Ferdindand Rodriquez, James Rollins, Raymond Schrump, Mark Smith, Richard Springman, Richard Utecht, Richard Waldhaus, Kenneth Wallingford, James Walsh, and George Wanat.

Chapter Twelve

Conditions in China

Official records show two Americans were shot down over China and held prisoner during the Vietnam War. Phillip Smith was shot down near Hai Nan island on 20 Sep 1965. He was held at Canton and then Beijing. Most of his time was spent in solitary confinement. Smith was released in Hong Kong on 15 Mar 1973. Robert Flynn was shot down along the Chinese-North Vietnamese border on 21 Aug 1967. He was held in Beijing and released on 15 Mar 1973 in Hong Kong.

Flynn was held at times with John Downey and at times with Richard Fectau, but the three were never together. Downey and Fectau were CIA officers shot down over Manchuria on 29 Nov 1952. They were held first at Mukden and then Beijing. After experiencing two years of lengthy interrogations, leg irons, and sleep deprivation, both men were convicted and sentenced. Downey was given life and Fectau twenty years.

Once they began serving their sentences they were allowed mail from home, one package a month from families, and monthly Red Cross packages. A few times family members were allowed to travel to China and visit. Reading material was available, sometimes even regular US publications. For a ten-year period regular "study sessions" were held by the Chinese. For a while in 1955 they were placed in the same cells as a B-29 crew (Stardust Four Zero, shot down over North Korea in January 1953) and allowed to believe they would all be released together. Other times privileges would be given and then abruptly removed. Their cells were cold and the windows covered. For one six year stretch they were kept in complete isolation. Even though they seldom saw each other they were able to communicate on rare occasions with coughs and notes written in the dust.

Fectau was released on 12 Dec 1971 and Downey was released on 12 Mar 1973. The more than twenty years John Downey spent as a prisoner would make him the longest- held American prisoner of any war.

Part IV

Chapter Thirteen

Escapes—Vietnam

In all the previous writings on the Vietnam War there does not seem to exist any one specific document listing the escapes and attempted escapes of American prisoners of war. That is the purpose of this chapter. It is not intended to be a detailed account of any specific escape or escapes. To find details of individual escapes use the sources listed in the bibliography. The larger number of escapes and escape attempts during the Korean War, and the minimal information available on those escapes, make a similar document close to impossible to create for Korea.

This first listing is of attempted escapes in Vietnam, escapes that did not lead to rescue, escapes that ended in recapture. The list is undoubtedly neither complete nor completely accurate. Neither the government nor the military has extensive information on most POWs from any war. Especially missing from this list are the attempts of those individuals for whom no record exists, those individuals who escaped before they arrived at a known camp, only to die from their wounds, beatings, executions, or the elements.

This list includes over ninety escape attempts, at least twenty of which took place in North Vietnam, five of them in Hanoi itself. There were American POWs who made multiple escape attempts.

No American POW escaped from North Vietnam and successfully reached friendly forces. American POWs did escape from camps in North Vietnam, some of them from camps in Hanoi. At least five escaped twice from camps in North Vietnam, some from established camps, others from guards while en-route to Hanoi. All of the men who escaped in North Vietnam were recaptured, usually, but not always, within the first day. At least one of them died from the torture which followed his recapture. One escape, which was planned to take place from the Hanoi Hilton, involved SR-71 Blackbirds flying overhead and Navy SEALs waiting at the mouth of the Red River. Senior Ranking Officers among the POWs canceled that attempt at the last minute.

In the European Theater of World War II less than two percent of American POWs successfully escaped and returned to US forces. In Vietnam more than four percent of American POWs successfully escaped and reached US forces. Factor in the completely foreign culture, language, and terrain and you begin to realize what this means. Those who tried deserve more recognition than they have ever been given.

Escapes and Attempts

Samuel Adams: USAF Sgt, captured near Vung Tau 31 Oct 65 with Dusing, Moore, and Page, escaped two days later with Jasper Page (South Vietnam), never seen again after escape. MIA.

Cloden Adkins: civilian captured in Hue during 68 Tet, held at Runamuck I, Skid Row, then Rock Pile. Escaped from Rock Pile (North Vietnam) in 1 Oct 71 with Thompson and Meyer. Adkins recaptured same day, Thompson and Meyer recaptured after about a day. Released in 1973.

John Thomas Anderson: USA Sgt, captured 5 Feb 68 in Hue. Held in North Vietnam. Three escape attempts, on first one he got a mile from camp and passed out from wounds, the second time he walked into an enemy camp, and the third time he was captured and beaten by villagers. Released in 1973.

Gerasimo Arroyo-Baez: USA Sgt, captured 24 Mar 69 in South Vietnam with Richard Bowers when their base near Saigon was overrun, escaped day of capture, recaptured later that day. Died in captivity. NVA list death as 22 Aug 1972.

Edwin Atterbury: USAF Capt, shot down 12 Aug 67 over North Vietnam. Escaped 10 May 69 from Zoo (outskirts of Hanoi, North Vietnam) with John Dramesi, recaptured same day. Died 18 May 69 in captivity as result of beatings/torture after his recapture.

Harold Bennett: USA Sgt, captured 29 Dec 64 in South Vietnam. Attempted escape in Mar 65 with Donald Cook, immediately recaptured. Last seen by fellow POWs 28 May 65. VC announced his execution in Jun 65. MIA.

Richard Bowers: USA Capt, captured 24 Mar 69 in South Vietnam with Arroyo-Baez when their base near Saigon was overrun, escaped day of capture. Killed by guards when recaptured several hours later.

Ernie Brace: ex-Marine civilian pilot captured in Laos 21 May 65, escaped that night (Laos), immediately recaptured. Escaped 6 Jun 65 for a few hours(Laos), recaptured. Escaped 17 Apr 66 and evaded for four days(North Vietnam), recaptured. Escaped 17 Aug 66 (North Vietnam), immediately recaptured, buried up to his chin for seven days, eventually sent to Hanoi. Released in 1973.

Harvey Brande: USA SFC, captured 7 Feb 68 at Lang Vei SF camp, escaped 18 Feb 68 with Dennis Thompson and evaded for seven days (South Vietnam), recaptured, taken to North Vietnam. Released in 1973.

Norman Brookens: AID civilian captured in Saigon 4 Feb 68 with Utecht, moved to camp in Cambodia. Attempted escape 22 Apr 68 with Richard Utecht, James Rollins, and Australian Charles K. Hyland, immediately recaptured. Released in 1973.

Richard Burgess: USMC L/Cpl, captured 25 Sep 66 in northern I Corps, attempted escape in early 67 (South Vietnam), recaptured, escaped with Riate in Aug 67 (South Vietnam) by tunneling under a wall, evaded for two days, sent to North Vietnam. Released in 1973.

Jack Butcher: USAF 1st Lt, shot down over Laos 24 Mar 71. Held in Laos six weeks. Escaped, recaptured after a few hours. While being taken to Hanoi Butcher escaped again. The second escape was made known to US forces from intercepted radio messages in Laos from NVA units looking for him. US rescue efforts were massive, including direct involvement of the Secretary of Defense. Recaptured after 10 days on the run, Butcher was told he would be shot if he tried it again. Released in 1973.

Carl Dennis Chambers: USAF 1st Lt, shot down over North Vietnam 7 Aug 67 with Glen Wilson. They escaped while en-route to Hanoi, attempted to steal two small boats, recaptured after 12 hours. Released in 1973.

Arvin Chauncey: USN Lt Cmdr, shot down over North Vietnam 31 May 67, escaped second night, recaptured. Released in 1973.

George Coker: USN Lt JG, shot down over North Vietnam 27 Aug 66, escaped the night of 12 Oct 67 with McKnight from Dirty Bird (Hanoi, North Vietnam), floated/swam approx 15 miles down river before recapture next day. Released in 1973.

Donald Cook: USMC Capt, captured 31 Dec 64 in South Vietnam. Attempted escape in March 65 with Harold Bennett, immediately recaptured. Died in captivity Dec 67. Awarded Medal of Honor for resistance as a POW.

George Day: USAF Maj, shot down 26 Aug 67 north of DMZ, captured, escaped shortly after (North Vietnam), evaded for two
weeks with a banged up leg and his right arm broken in three
places. He had crossed the DMZ back into South Vietnam
where he was shot as he was recaptured. Awarded Medal of
Honor for escape and resistance as a POW. Released in 1973.

Eugene Debruin: civilian with Air America captured 5 Sep 63 in Laos
when C-46 was shot down, escaped May 64 with others for four
days (Laos), recaptured. Escaped 29 Jun 66 again (Laos) with
Dengler and Martin. Debruin not seen after escape. MIA.

Joe DeLong: USA Pvt, captured 18 May 67 in Cambodia or South
Vietnam. Attempted escape from camp in Cambodia Nov 67
with Perricone and Sooter. Probably killed in attempt. MIA.

Dieter Dengler: USN Lt JG, shot down 1 Feb 66 in Laos, evaded one
day, captured. Escaped mid Feb 66 (Laos), recaptured that
same day. On 29 Jun 66 escaped with Debruin and Martin.
Evaded three weeks, rescued by US forces 20 Jul 66.

John Dramesi: USAF Capt, shot down over North Vietnam 2 Apr 67,
escaped (North Vietnam) 10 Apr 67 while being transported to
Hanoi, evaded one day, escaped 10 May 69 from Zoo (outskirts
of Hanoi, North Vietnam) with Edwin Atterbury, evaded 12
hours before recapture. Released in 1973.

Yves-Michel Dumond: French journalist captured at Loc Ninh 7 Apr 72
with American advisors. Escaped for two days in May while
held in Cambodia. Released 13 July 72.

William Eisenbraun: USA Capt, captured 5 Jul 65 in South Vietnam.
Two escape attempts in all. Attempted escape with Russell
Grissett in early fall 67. Died in captivity Sep 67, possibly as a
result of beating for escape attempt.

Walter Ferguson Jr: USA PFC, captured 23 Aug 68 in South Vietnam,
moved to camp in or near Cambodia. POWs held with him believe he was killed in an escape attempt in summer 1970.

Carroll Flora: USA E6, captured 21 Jul 67 in South Vietnam. Awarded
Silver Star for escape while a POW. No further info found. Released from Hanoi in 1973.

George Fryett: USA Spec 4, captured 24 Dec 61 in Saigon, attempted
    escaped shortly after (South Vietnam), recaptured. Released 24
    June 1962.
John Graf: USN Lt Cmdr, shot down 15 Nov 69 over South Vietnam.
    Pilot captured with Graf reported Graf attempted escaped in late
    Jan 1970. Believed to have been killed in that attempt. Listed
    as MIA.
Joseph Grainger: USAID civilian captured 8 Aug 64. Escaped 5 Jan
    65, killed while being re-captured a week later.
Robert Greer: USMC PFC, captured 7 Jun 64 near Da Nang in South
    Vietnam, attempted escape shortly after with Schreckengost.
    Some reports say he was killed in escape attempt. MIA.
Edwin Russell Grissett: USMC LCpl, captured 22 Jan 66 in South
    Vietnam. Attempted escape, recaptured. Attempted second es-
    cape in early fall 67 with William Eisenbraun, recaptured. Died
    in captivity the day before Thanksgiving Nov 68.
Dennis Hammond: USMC Cpl, captured 8 Feb 68 with Joseph Zaw-
    tocki, escaped Apr 68 with Weatherman while at Kushner Camp
    near Tam Ky (South Vietnam) by taking weapon from guard,
    shot in the leg by villagers and recaptured. Placed in stocks
    and beaten daily for two weeks (or two months). Died in cap-
    tivity March 1970.
William Hardy: USA Capt, captured 29 Jun 1967 near Saigon in South
    Vietnam. Awarded Silver Star for escape attempt during August
    1967. Released in 1973.
David Harker: USA PFC, captured 8 Jan 68 in South Vietnam. Es-
    caped shortly after capture, suffered knife wound in recapture.
    Released in 1973.
Douglas Hegdahl: USN E2, captured 6 Mar 67 in the South China Sea
    after being blown overboard from the USS Canberra. At-
    tempted escape in Aug 68 (North Vietnam) while being used to
    film a version of his capture. Ordered to accept early release 4
    Aug 69.

Charles Keith Hyland. Australian civilian captured 6 Feb 68. Escaped
    for a very brief period in February or March before being recap-
    tured. This escape occurred in either South Vietnam or Cambo-
    dia. Attempted escape 22 Apr 68 with Richard Utecht, James
    Rollins, and Norman Brookens, immediately recaptured. Re-
    leased on 26 Nov 68.
Charles Jackson: USAF Capt, shot down 24 Jun 72 over North Viet-
    nam and captured, escaped, recaptured. Released in 1973.
Bobby Johnson: USA E-4, captured 25 Aug 68. Attempted escape in
    1970 or 1971 while held in the Parrot's Beak area. May have
    been across the border in Cambodia at the time. Released in
    1973.
Wilson Denver Key: USN Lt, shot down 17 Nov 67 near Hanoi. Es-
    caped from back of truck and made it into the Red River,
    evaded for an hour before recapture. Released in 1973.
Arthur Krause: civilian captured 8 Jun 63. Reportedly escaped 23 June
    and evaded for two weeks. Recaptured. Released 18 Nov 63.
James Latham: USAF Capt, shot down over southern North Vietnam 5
    Oct 72. Escaped early Nov 72, recaptured after six hours. Re-
    leased in 1973.
Don MacPhail: USA E3, captured 8 Feb 69 twelve miles northwest of
    Pleiku. Two escape attempts while held in Cambodia. Released
    in 1973.
Duane Martin: USAF 1st Lt, helicopter shot down 20 Sep 65 on border
    of North Vietnam and Laos, evaded two weeks, captured. Es-
    caped 29 Jun 66 with Dengler and Debruin (Laos). Evaded
    with Dengler two weeks. Killed by villagers as they evaded.
George McKnight: USAF Capt, shot down 6 Nov 65 over North Viet-
    nam, escaped with Coker from Dirty Bird 12 Oct 67 (Hanoi,
    North Vietnam), got approx 15 miles down river, recaptured
    next day. Released in 1973.
Lewis Meyer: civilian captured 1 Feb 68 in Hue during Tet, escaped
    from Rock Pile (North Vietnam) 1 Oct 71 with Thompson and
    Adkins, recaptured with Thompson after about a day. Released
    in 1973.

Thomas Moe: USAF 1st Lt, aircraft damaged from faulty bomb fuses, bailed out 16 Jan 68 over Laos. Evaded for three days. Escaped twice in first few days of capture, immediately recaptured. Released in 1973.

Walter H. Moon: USA Capt, captured 22 Apr 61 in Laos. Made two escape attempts which, along with his refusal to cooperate, led to his execution 22 Jul 1961.

Stanley Newell: USA E4, captured 12 Jul 67 near Pleiku. Escape attempt in South Vietnam. Released in 1973.

Michael O'Connor: USA WO, captured 4 Feb 68. Attempted escape before arriving at Portholes in North Vietnam. Released in 1973.

Richard Perricone: USA PFC, captured 12 Jul 67 near Pleiku in South Vietnam. Attempted escape from camp in Cambodia Nov 67 with DeLong and Sooter, recaptured same day. Released in 1973.

Robert Phillips: USA Pvt, captured 23 Jun 70 in South Vietnam. Reportedly killed in escape attempt with Rozo, date unknown. MIA.

Dan Pitzer: USA Sgt, captured 29 Oct 63 in the Mekong Delta with Rowe and Versace. Attempted escape 23 Dec 64 with Rowe during an American raid on the area , quickly recaptured. Released 11 Nov 67.

Ben Purcell: USA Col, shot down over South Vietnam (helicopter) on 8 Feb 68, taken to North Vietnam. Escaped 7 Dec 69 from Skid Row (North Vietnam). Worked for three months to remove part of cell door. Headed into Hanoi, hitching a ride on the back of a bicycle. Recaptured next day. Escaped from Mountain Camp (North Vietnam) on 18 Mar 72, evaded just over a day, recaptured. Released in 1973.

James Michael Ray: USA PFC, captured 18 Mar 68 in South Vietnam. Awarded Silver Star for escape attempt in Jul 69. Credited with two escape attempts. Reportedly died in captivity 6 Nov 69. MIA.

King Rayford: USA PFC, captured 2 Jul 67 in South Vietnam. Escaped with Ray Ziegler on 18 Feb 68 (South Vietnam), recaptured next day. Released in 1973.

Alfonso Riate: USMC Corp, captured 26 Apr 67, escaped with Burgess in Aug 67 (South Vietnam), evaded for two days, recaptured. Released in 1973.

William Reeder: USA Capt, captured 9 May 72 in South Vietnam. Made escape attempt while being moved on foot from Cambodia to North Vietnam. Released in 1973.

James Rollins: civilian captured 4 or 5 Feb 68 near Saigon in South Vietnam, attempted escape from camp in Cambodia with Richard Utecht, Charles Hyland, and Norman Brookens on 22 Apr 68, immediately recaptured. Released in 1973.

James (Nick) Rowe: USA 1st Lt, captured 29 Oct 63 in Mekong Delta with Pitzer and Versace. Attempted escape 23 Dec 64 with Pitzer during an American raid on the area , quickly recaptured. Escaped late at night Oct 65 with Tadios, recaptured next morning. Early 68 Rowe simply walked away from his camp but walked into a regular VC camp. He convinced everyone he was lost while looking for firewood. Fall 68 he attempted to reach a main canal and flag down a plane. Was able to convince guards he was simply fishing. Successfully escaped 31 Dec 68.

James Rozo: USA Spec 4th, captured 23 Jun 70 in South Vietnam. Reportedly killed in escape attempt with Phillips, date unknown. MIA.

Fred Schreckengost: USMC PFC, captured 7 Jun 64 in South Vietnam, attempted escape shortly after with Greer. May have been killed in escape attempt or later may have been collaborator, part of Salt and Pepper team. Evidence is not clear either way. Remains identified 1991.

John Sexton: USA Corporal, captured 12 Aug 69. Attempted escape with Springman in 1970 or 1971 while held in the Parrot's Beak area. May have been across the border in Cambodia at the time. Released in Oct 1971.

Charles Shelton: USAF Capt, shot down over Laos 29 Apr 65. Made at least three escape attempts in Laos. MIA.

Lance Sijan: USAF 1st Lt, shot down 9 Nov 67 in Laos, evaded capture after bail out for 46 days. Captured 26 Dec 67, escaped, immediately recaptured, died from his injuries in captivity 22 Jan 68. Awarded the Medal of Honor for his actions while a POW.

James Simpson: Civilian captured 5 Nov 68 in South Vietnam with
British civilian Thomas Cornthwaite. Both killed in escape attempt shortly after.

David Sooter: USA CWO 1, captured 17 Feb 67 in South Vietnam. Attempted escape from camp in Cambodia Nov 67 with DeLong
and Perricone, recaptured same day. Released in 1973.

Richard Springman: USA E4, captured 25 May 70. Attempted escape with
Sexton in 1970 or 1971 while held in the Parrot's Beak area. May
have been across the border in Cambodia at the time. Released in
1973.

Len Tadios: USA Sgt, captured 11 Dec 64 in Mekong Delta, escaped
Jun 65, recaptured after 3 days. Escaped late at night Oct 65
with Rowe, recaptured next morning. Died Mar 66 in captivity.
(Called Davila in Rowe's book *Five Years to Freedom*.)

Dennis Thompson: USA SSgt, captured 7 Feb 68 when Lang Vei SF
camp overrun. He made two escape attempts as he was moved
to a temporary camp in Laos, severely beaten. Escaped 18 Feb
68 (Laos) with Brande, evaded 7 days, at times carrying Brande
piggyback. Recaptured 25 Feb 68. Attempted escape again, recaptured immediately and beaten almost to death. Released in
1973.

Floyd (James) Thompson: USA Capt, captured 26 Mar 64 south of
DMZ, moved to camp in Laos. Three escape attempts in first
month of captivity, each time convincing guards who discovered him he was only leaving camp area to urinate. A fourth attempt was made in May or June. The fifth attempt was on 21
Jul 64, recaptured later that day. Escaped again 1 Oct 71 from
Rock Pile (North Vietnam) with Meyer and Adkins, recaptured
after about a day with Meyer. Longest held American POW of
Vietnam War. Released in 1973.

Richard Utecht: Civilian captured in Saigon 4 Feb 68 with Brookens,
moved to camp in Cambodia. Attempted escape 22 Apr 68 with
Norman Brookens, Charles Hyland, and James Rollins, immediately recaptured. Released in 1973.

Thomas Van Putten: USA Cpl, captured 11 Feb 68 in South Vietnam.
Made two attempts before his final successful escape March of
1969. He evaded for three weeks before being spotted by helicopters.

Humberto Versace: USA Capt, captured 29 Oct 63 in Mekong Delta
with Pitzer and Rowe. Attempted escape late Nov 63, immediately recaptured. Medal of Honor citation lists 3 escape attempts. Other sources say there were five attempts. The
VC/National Liberation Front announced he had been executed
on 26 Sep 65. In 2002 he was posthumously awarded the
Medal of Honor for his actions while a POW, even though the
original recommendation had been submitted thirty three years
prior.

Orien J Walker, Jr: USA Capt, captured 23 May 65 in Mekong Delta
area. Escaped shortly capture, recaptured. Died in captivity
Feb 66. (Called Tim Barker in Rowe's book *Five Years to Freedom*.)

Earl Weatherman: USA PFC, captured or defected 8 Nov 67 near Da
Nang in South Vietnam. Escaped Apr 68 with Hammond from
Kushner Camp near Tam Ky (South Vietnam), quickly recaptured, executed by villagers. Some fellow POWs had some
doubts if death actually happened, considered Weatherman a
collaborator. Others say he was killed by the villagers in the escape attempt. Not listed as a POW.

Glen Wilson: USAF Capt, shot down over North Vietnam 7 Aug 67
with Carl Dennis Chambers. They escaped while en-route to
Hanoi, attempted to steal two small boats, recaptured after 12
hours. Released in 1973.

Roy Ziegler: USA CWO 1, captured 8 Feb 68 when helicopter shot
down in South Vietnam. Escaped 18 Feb 68 (South Vietnam)
with King Rayford, recaptured next day. Released in 1973.

Successful Escapes

All escapes were in South Vietnam unless otherwise noted

Thirty-three American prisoners of war escaped and then reached U.S. forces. Of those thirty-three successful attempts, twenty-eight of them occurred within the first month of captivity. Only three successful escapes took place after the prisoners had been held more than a year, each of them in the South.

Donald R. Braswell, USA E4, was captured 23 Aug 1967 and escaped 24 Aug 1967 with civilian Dewey Holt.

Lee Brewer, USA E5, captured 7 Jan 1968 and escaped 8 Jan.

Issac Camacho, USA SFC, was captured west of Saigon on 24 Nov 1963 along with Claude McClure, Kenneth Roraback, and George Smith when the Hiep Hoa SF camp west of Saigon was overrun. On 12 Jul 1965 Camacho escaped during a night rainstorm and made it to US forces. The others helped cover his escape. Camacho was the first US military POW to escape.

Dieter Dengler, Lt JG USN, was shot down 1 Feb 1966 over Laos while flying an A1H off the USS Ranger. He evaded until 2 Feb. On 29 Jun he escaped with other POWs. On 20 July he was able to signal US aircraft and was rescued.

Edward A. Dierling, USA E5, captured in Hue 1 Feb 1968 and escaped 23 Feb 1968 with Hayhurst near the Laotian border.

Joe L. Dodd, civilian, was captured 8 Oct 1965. Successfully escaped 25 Oct.

James Dodson, USMC E3, was captured 6 May 1966 near Da Nang and escaped 17 Jun 1966 when he and Walter Eckes grabbed the guards' rifles while they were eating and escaped. They reached US forces four days after the escape.

Walter W. Eckes, USMC E3, was captured 10 May 1966 near Da Nang. On 17 Jun 1966 he and James Dodson grabbed the guards' rifles while they were eating and escaped. They reached US forces four days after the escape.

Jerry L. Fann, USA, captured 21 Mar 1967 and escaped 21 Mar 1967.

Bruce A. Graening, USA E3, captured 9 Mar 1967, escaped 18 Mar.

Kenneth R. Gregory, USA E6, captured 25 Aug 1968. He was found by a US helicopter on 26 May 1969 four days after his escape. He reported he had been scheduled for release if he signed a propaganda statement, but escaped the day before that was to happen. Listed in some sources as released.

Jerry L. Guffey, USA E4, captured 4 Mar 1969 and escaped 4 Mar.

Walter D. Hamilton, USMC Pvt, captured 18 Oct 1965 near Da Nang and escaped 29 October, along with Joseph North, Jr.

Paul G. Hatch, USA E3, captured 24 Aug 1969 and escaped 25 Aug.

Robert E. Hayhurst, USA E5, captured in Hue 1 Feb 1968 and escaped 23 Feb with Dierling near the Laotian border.

Dewey T. Holt, civilian or USA E4, was captured 23 Aug 1967 and escaped 24 Aug 1967 with Donald Braswell.

Frank C. Iodice, USMC Cpl, captured with Albert Potter 30 May 1968. Both escaped 1 June during an attack by ARVN forces.

Everett M. King Jr, USA E4, captured 1 Feb 1968 in Hue with Dierling and Hayhurst. Wounded, unable to walk, hid from his NVA captors in rubble on 8 Feb and managed to contact a US patrol on 9 Feb.

Charles Klusmann, USN Lt, Flying an RF8A from the USS Kitty Hawk, forced to bail out over Laos 6 Jun 1964. He and two Lao soldiers escaped the night of 30 August and reached friendly forces on 1 September.

Donald E. Martin, USA Spec 5, captured 2 Mar 1968 and escaped 15 Apr.

Steven D. Nelson, USMC Corp, captured 7 Jan 1968 with Michael Roha. Both escaped 21 Jan, reaching US forces the next day.

Joseph S. North, Jr, USMC Pvt, captured 18 Oct 1965 near Da Nang and escaped 29 October, along with Walter Hamilton.

Jasper Page , USAF SSgt, captured 31 Oct 1965 near Vung Tau. Escaped several nights later with Samuel Adams when they jumped their guards. Adams was killed. Page made it to US forces on 4 Nov.

Albert J. Potter, USMC Sgt, captured with Frank Iodice 30 May 1968. Both escaped 1 June during an attack by ARVN forces.

Richard F. Risner, USMC Maj, captured 20 Aug 1968 and escaped 22
    Aug.
Michael R. Roha, USMC Pfc, captured 7 Jan 1968 with Steven Nelson.
    Both escaped 21 Jan, reaching US forces the next day.
James (Nick) Rowe, USA 1st Lt, captured 29 Oct 1963 in the Mekong
    Delta area. After four escape attempts he successfully escaped
    on 31 Dec 1968 while US forces were bombing the area. He
    managed to flag down a helicopter which almost fired upon him
    before they spotted his white skin and beard.
Linda Smith, civilian captured with Michelle Smith 10 Mar 1975 and
    escaped 27 Mar.
Michelle L. Smith, civilian captured with Linda Smith 10 Mar 1975
    and escaped 27 Mar.
William P. Taliaferro, USMC E4, captured 4 Feb 1968 and escaped 12
    Feb. Also spelled Tallaferno. (He may have been released.)
William B. Taylor, USA Spec 5, captured 20 Mar 1968 when the O1D
    he was an observer in was shot down. On 6 May 1968 US heli-
    copters attacked the camp he was held in without knowing he
    was there. Taylor had been severely injured in the crash of his
    plane. He was wounded again by the US attack. He crawled to
    a clearing and caught the attention of a US helicopter. When it
    came in he grabbed the skid but was shot off. The helicopter re-
    turned and the crew threw him aboard. He would not have been
    rescued if he had not first escaped on his own during the attack.
Thomas H. Van Putten, USA Cpl, captured 10 Feb 1968 and escaped 29
    Mar 1969, evaded for three weeks before he was able to wave
    down a helicopter.
Buddy Wright, USA Sgt, captured 22 Sep 1968 while on a long-range
    reconnaissance patrol in Cambodia. Escaped and evaded for 10
    days, finally reaching US forces 6 Oct.

Chapter Fourteen

Successful Rescues

There were only five Americans actually rescued from captivity during the entire war. One died shortly after rescue from wounds inflicted by his guards before they ran from the rescue forces. This was the only intended rescue. The others were unplanned rescues. One took place while the prisoner was being escorted from his point of capture to a prison camp. Another involved a helicopter assault in an area which turned out to hold prisoners. An American POW broke loose and ran to the helicopters. Two American civilians were accidentally rescued when their captors ran into an American ambush. There were many attempts to rescue American POWs, the most well known being the attack on the camp at Son Tay in North Vietnam. There were at least 45 raids aimed specifically at rescuing American POWs. After the war there were cases where prisoners reported they had been within sight and sound of American rescue forces but were prevented by their guards from taking any action. There were about five hundred South Vietnamese soldiers freed in these rescue attempts. Some American politicians and senior officers involved in the decision making for rescue efforts of American POWs hindered those efforts more than they helped.

Larry D. Aiken, USA E4, captured 13 May 1969. A Vietnamese reported seeing him in a VC hospital complex. A raid was carried out on 10 Jul 1969 to rescue Aiken. He was found outside the hut he had been seen in, suffering a fresh head wound. He was rescued but remained in a coma from the head wound until his death on 25 July. Aiken's recovery was the only "successful" planned rescue of an American POW during the entire war.

Roger D. Anderson, USA Pvt, captured 3 Jan 1968 about 65 miles
    south of Saigon. This may be the only planned rescue attempt
    that actually succeeded, even then it was accidental in the end.
    About five days after his capture an agent reported seeing An-
    derson being marched away from the area by a column of VC.
    Helicopter units were told to search towards Cambodia. On 12
    Jan a helicopter pilot spotted a sampan with two men. When he
    buzzed them they gave him reason to open fire. One VC was
    killed. Anderson jumped up from the bottom of the sampan and
    took off his uniform shirt so they could see he was an American.
Henry Hudson, civilian, captured 21 Dec 1965. Later that same night
    an American unit ambushed the group as they were being
    marched through the jungle. Hudson, fellow civilian Edwin
    Jones, and their Vietnamese driver were rescued. Canadian
    Otto Shulten was killed by the guards.
Edwin Jones, civilian, captured 21 Dec 1965. Later that same night an
    American unit ambushed the group as they were being marched
    through the jungle. Jones, fellow civilian Henry Hudson, and
    their Vietnamese driver were rescued. Canadian Otto Shulten
    was killed by the guards.
William B. Taylor, USA Spec 5, captured 20 Mar 1968 when the O1D
    he was an observer in was shot down. On 6 May 1968 US heli-
    copters attacked the camp he was held in without knowing he
    was there. Taylor had been severely injured in the crash of his
    plane. He was wounded again by the US attack. He crawled to
    a clearing and caught the attention of a US helicopter. When it
    came in he grabbed the skid but was shot off. The helicopter re-
    turned and the crew threw him aboard. He would not have been
    rescued if he had not first escaped on his own during the attack.
    He is listed on the escape list above.

Chapter Fifteen

American Women Held as POWs

Evelyn Anderson was captured 27 Oct 1972 with Beatrice Kosin while working as a missionary near Savannakhet, Laos. Five days later she was burned alive in the hut she was held in. The two men captured with her were sent on to Hanoi and released there.

Beatrice Kosin was captured 27 Oct 1972 with Evelyn Anderson while working as a missionary near Savannakhet, Laos. Five days later she was burned alive in the hut she was held in. The two men captured with her were sent on to Hanoi and released there.

Ofelia Gaza was captured near Vung Tau in June of 1966 with her husband Vincente. He worked for Air America and may not have been an American citizen. Vincente Gaza died in December 1966 and his wife Ofelia was released the beginning of January 1967. Neither are on the DPMO listing.

Sandra Johnson was captured on 5 Feb 68 in Hue along with Marjorie Nelson. They were held at what was later called Camp Runamuck near Phu Bai. They were released on 31 Mar 68.

Dr. Marjorie Nelson was captured on 5 Feb 68 in Hue along with Sandra Johnson. They were held at what was later called Camp Runamuck near Phu Bai. They were released on 31 Mar 68.

Betty Ann Olsen, a nurse working at Ban Me Thout, Olsen was captured during Tet on 1 Feb 68. The group of POWs she was held with was moved constantly back and forth across the border into Cambodia. Olsen contracted malaria, beri beri, and dysentery. She died in captivity in Sep 68.

Elizabeth Pond, a journalist, was captured in Cambodia with Michael Morrow and Richard Dudman in May of 1970. All were released in June.

Linda Smith, civilian captured 10 Mar 75 and escaped either 21 or 27 Mar 75.

Michelle L. Smith, civilian captured 10 Mar 75 and escaped either 21 or 27 Mar 75.

Eleanor Vietti was captured/kidnapped at the leprosarium at Bon Me Thout 30 May 62 along with Daniel Gerber and Archie Mitchell. All remain MIA.

Cathy Leroy (France), and Michele Ray (France), Kate Webb (Australia or New Zealand) also spent time as prisoners and were released.

Chapter Sixteen

POW Anomalies

Orville Frits: USA Sgt, captured 20 May 67 with Grammar, tortured and killed. Not listed as a POW.

William Grammar: USMC 1st Lt, captured 20 May 67 with Frits, tortured and killed. Not listed as a POW. Frits and Grammar were not killed in action. Their bodies showed obvious signs of torture prior to their deaths. They were prisoners of war when they died.

Frank Prendergast: USN Lt JG, shot down over North Vietnam 9 Mar 67, Prendergast landed off shore in the surf and was captured by two North Vietnamese soldiers. Prendergast shot one and exchanged shots with the other while the rescue helicopter approached. The rescue helicopter shot the soldier and picked up Prendergast. He is not listed as a POW.

Doyle Morgan USA, Leonard Sroveck USA, Ciro Salas USAF, Giacomo Appice USAF, and Jerry Schuller USAF, were captured near Da Nang on 14 Jun 1954 by the Viet Minh. They were apparently thought by the Viet Minh to have been French troops. They were held in a POW camp with French POWs and were released on 31 Aug 1954. They do not appear on some official listings of American POWs in Vietnam.

Charles Shelton and David Hrdlicka may have been rescued in Laos by a native team. Sources indicate this team attempted to bring them out, acting as a Pathet Lao unit which had captured the two Americans. While doing so they encountered a North Vietnamese unit which reminded the "Pathet Lao" soldiers that all prisoners were to be turned over to the North Vietnamese. To protect both the POWs and the native team, and with the supposed agreement of both Shelton and Hrdlicka, this was done. Further rescue attempts were impossible. Both remain MIA.

Information on these two individuals, as with most MIA from Laos, is confused by US government records as much as any other factor.

An Air Force pilot captured on 20 Dec 67 took part in a one of a kind escape attempt. Robert Craner was shot down while flying as a Misty Fac over North Vietnam with Guy Gruters. As rescue efforts took place on 21 Dec Craner began talking to pilots overhead saying he was captured but was in a dialogue with his captors about trading him for a gold reward. Authentication proved it was actually Craner. This discussion continued with rescue aircraft overhead as they marched Craner north, at times one of the North Vietnamese soldiers talking on the radio. Gold bars were actually obtained and in a helicopter off-shore the next morning. When radio contact was made in an effort to arrange a pick-up point one of the North Vietnamese stated Craner could be picked up in Hanoi and communication was cut off. Both Craner and Gruters were released in 1973.

Bibliography I - Korea

Bassett, Richard M. *And the Wind Blew Cold.* Kent State University Press: Kent, Ohio, 2002.

Biderman, Albert D. *March to Calumny.* The Macmillan Company: New York, 1963.

Carlson, Lewis H. *Remembered Prisoners of a Forgotten War.* St. Martin's Griffin: New York, 2002.

Chapman, Jack. Personal communications.

Cole, Paul M. *POW/MIA* Issues Vol 1, The Korean War. RAND: Santa Monica, CA, 1994.

Cortez, Oscar. Personal communications.

Cram, Bruce. Personal communications.

Crosbie, Philip. *Pencilling Prisoner.* The Hawthorn Press: Melbourne, Australia, 1955.

Cunningham, Cyril. *No Mercy, No Leniency.* Redwood Books: Trowbridge, Wiltshire, England, 2000.

Davies, S. J. *In Spite of Dungeons.* Bath Press: Bat, Avon, England, 1954.

Estabrook, Wilbert. Personal communications.

Farrar-Hockley, Anthony. *The Edge of the Sword.* The Companion Book Club: London, 1955.

Gaston, Peter. *Korea 1950-1953 Prisoners of War The British Army.* Lightning Source UK Ltd: United Kingdom, 1976.

Green, David. *Captured at the Imjin River.* Pen and Sword Books Ltd: South Yorkshire, England, 2003.

Hackworth, David C. *About Face.* Touchstone: New York, 1989.

Jones, Francis S. *No Rice For Rebels.* Transworld Publishers Ltd: London, 1957.

JPAC June 2006 update www.koreanwarexpow.org

Lech, Raymond B. *Broken Soldiers.* University of Illinois Press: Urbana and Chicago, 2000.

Leerkamp, Henry. Personal communications.

MacDonald, James Angus. *The Problem of U.S. Marine Corps Prisoners of War in Korea.* History and Museums Division HQ, US Marine Corps: Washington D.C. 1962.

Maher, William L. *A Shepherd in Combat Boots*. Beidel Printing
    House, Inc: Shippensburg, PA. 1997.
Norton, Bruce H. and Maffioli, Len. *Grown Gray in War*. Ballantine
    Books: New York, 1997.
Page, William Frank. *The Health of Former Prisoners of War*. National
    Academy Press: Washington, D.C. 1992
Pate, Lloyd W. *Reactionary*-Revised 2000. Vantage Press, Inc: New
    York, 2001.
POW... the fight continues... A report by the Secretary of Defense's Ad-
    visory Committee on Prisoners of War. Aug 1955.
POW Debriefs, Record Group 153, National Archives and Records Ad-
    ministration, College Park, Maryland, through Korean War
    POW/MIA Network.
Rowley, Arden A. *Korea-POW*. Tanner Publishing: Mesa, Arizona,
    1997.
Rowley, Arden A. *U.S. Prisoners of War in the Korean War*. Turner
    Publishing Co: Paducah, Kentucky, 2002.
Selby, Charles. Personal communications.
Shadish, William R. and Carlson, Lewis H. *When Hell Froze Over*.
    iUniverse, Inc: New York 2007.
U.S. Senate. Committee on Government Operations. *Korean War
    Atrocities*. Senate Report No. 848. 83rd Congress. 11 January
    1954. Washington D.C.
Touey, John. Personal communications.
White, William Lindsay. *The Captives of Korea*. Charles Scribner's
    Sons: New York, 1957.
Zellers, Larry. *In Enemy Hands*. The University Press of Kentucky:
    Lexington, Kentucky, 1991.

Bibliography II
Vietnam, Cambodia, Laos, and China

Advocacy and Intelligence Index for Prisoners of War-Missing in Action

Anton, Frank and Tommy Denton. *Why Didn't You Get Me Out?* Arlington, TX: Summit Publishing Group, 1997.

Badua, Candido. *Our Story.* www.baduanet

Blakey, Scott. *Prisoner of War, The Survival of Commander Richard A. Stratton.* New York: Anchor Press/Doubleday, 1978.

Brace, Ernest C. *A Code To Keep.* New York: St. Martin's Press, 1988.

Coffee, Gerald. *Beyond Survival, Building on the Hard Times-A POW's Inspiring Story.* New York: G.P. Putnam's Sons, 1990.

Daly, James and Bergman, Lee. *A Hero's Welcome.* Indianapolis, New York: Bobbs-Merrill Company, 1975.

Day, George E. *Return With Honor.* Mesa, AZ: Champlin Museum Press, 1989

Day, George E. *The Seventh Annual Hugh J. Clausen Lecture on Leadership to the 49th Judge Advocate Officer Graduate Course at the Judge Advocate General's School.* U.S. Army, Charlottesville, Virginia, 26 March 2001.

Defense POW/Missing Personnel Office (DPMO). Vietnam War missing personnel report.

Dockery, Kevin. *Operation Thunderhead.* New York: Berkley Publishing Group, 2008.

Dujmovic, Nicholas. *Two CIA Prisoners in China, 1952-73.* Available at https://www.cia.gov/library/center-for-the-study-of-intelligence

Guarino, Larry. *A POW's Story.* New York: Ballantine Books, 1990.

Hall, George and Pat, with Pittman, Bob. *Commitment to Honor.* Jackson, MS: Franklin Printers, 2005.

Hayhurst, Robert E. personal correspondence, June 2008.

Hirsch, James S. *Two Souls Indivisible.* New York: Houghton Mifflin Company, 2004.

Howes, Craig. *Voices of the Vietnam POWs.* Oxford Univ Press, 1993.

Hubbell, John G. *P.O.W., A Definitive History of the American Prisoner-of-War Experience in Vietnam.* 1964-1973. New York: Reader's Digest Press, 1976.

Karnow, Stanley. *Vietnam: A History.* New York: Viking Press, 1983.

Kushner, Hal. Speech to 1st Cav Reunion,
http://members.aol.com/bear317/kushner.htm

Library of Congress, Federal Research Division, POW/MIA Databases & Documents, Vietnam-Era POW/MIA Database, Washington, D.C.

Microsoft Encarta On-line Encyclopedia 2004, "Prisoners of War (POWs)"

McCain, John with Mark Salter. *Faith of My Fathers.* New York: Random House, 1999.

McConnell, Malcolm with Theodore Schweitzer III. *Inside Hanoi's Secret Archives – Solving the MIA Mystery.* New York: Simon and Schuster, 1995.

Peterson, Lowell. *The Birds Were Silver Then.* Appleton, Wisconsin: Peterson House, 2006.

Philpott, Tom. *Glory Denied, The Saga of Jim Thompson, America's Longest-Held Prisoner of War.* New York: W.W. Norton, 2001.

Plumb, Charlie. *I'm No Hero.* Independence Press, 1973.

Powell, Stewart M. *Honor Bound, Air Force, Journal of the Air Force Association*, August 1999, Vol. 82, No.8.

Pownetwork.org/bios.htmpowmiaff.org/Dumond

Purcell, Ben and Anne. *Love & Duty.* Thorndike, Maine: Thorndike Press, 1992.

Return With Honor. PBS On-line transcript with George Day and Ed Mechenbier, 9 Nov 2000.

Risner, Robinson. *The Passing of the Night. My Seven Years As a Prisoner of the North Vietnamese.* New York: Random House, 1973.

Rochester, Stuart and Frederick Kiley. *Honor Bound, American Prisoners of War in Southeast Asia 1961-1973.* Annapolis: Naval Institute Press, 1998.

Rowan, Stephen A. *They Wouldn't Let Us Die, The Prisoners of War Tell Their Story.* Middle Village, New York: Jonathon David Publishers, 1973.

Rowe, James N. *Five Years to Freedom.* Ballantine Books, 1971.

Rutledge, Howard and Phyllis. *In the Presence Of Mine Enemies.* Boston: Fleming H. Revell Company, 1973.

Schemmer, Benjamin F. *The Raid, The Son Tay Prison Rescue Mission*. New York: Ballantine Books, 1976.

Schwinn, Monicka and Diehl, Bernhard. *We Came To Help*. New York and London: Harcourt Brace Jovanovich, 1976.

Sheehan, Neil. *A Bright and Shining Lie: John Paul Vann and America in Vietnam*. New York: Vintage Books, 1988.

Skelton, William P. III. American EX-POW Lecture Series, *Presumptive Service Connected Disabilities*.

Smith, George E. *P.O.W. Two Years With The Vietcong*. Berkeley, California: Ramparts Press, 1971.

Stockstill, Louis R. *Prisoners of War-The Forgotten Americans of the Vietnam War, Air Force*. Journal of the Air Force Association, October 1969, Vol. 52, No. 10.

Thorsness, Leo. *Surviving Hell*. New York: Encounter Books, 2008.

Veith, George J. *Code-Name Bright Light, The Untold Story of U.S. POW Rescue Efforts During the War*. New York: Dell Publishing, 1998.

Vinson, Beth W. *To Hell and Beyond*. Minneapolis, MN: Mill City Press, Inc, 2008.

Wagaman, Winnie and Brookens, Norman J. *Civilian POW: Terror and Torture in South Vietnam*. Hagerstown, Maryland:Warm Welcomes Design & Publications, 1989.

Index

About the Author:

John N. Powers was the youngest enlisted man on the intelligence team at Phu Cat that briefed Major George Day on the morning of the day he was shot down and captured. He was involved in the authentication process for Major Robert Craner on the day he and Captain Guy Gruters were shot down and captured. His wife's father, USMC Platoon Sergeant Harold A. Hoffman, was captured in China on 8 Dec 1941 and spent until 15 Sep 1945 as slave labor in China and Japan.

Powers earned a BS and MST degree from the University of Wisconsin-Stevens Point and taught for 31 years. He serves as a historian for the North China Marines and is the creator and web master of www.northchinamarines.com. Powers considers that web site and this book to be a continuation of his teaching career - with a much larger classroom.

Made in the USA
Columbia, SC
14 February 2018